LOVING HOMOSEXUALS AS JESUS WOULD

LOVING HOMOSEXUALS AS JESUS WOULD

A *Fresh* Christian Approach

CHAD W. THOMPSON

Published by Brazos Press
a division of Baker Publishing Group
P.O. Box 6287, Grand Rapids, MI 49516-6287
www.brazospress.com

Printed in the United States of America

Library of Congress Cataloging-in-Publication Data
Thompson, Chad W., 1979–
Loving homosexuals as Jesus would : a fresh Christian approach / Chad W. Thompson.
p. cm.
Includes bibliographical references.
ISBN 1-58743-121-1 (pbk.)
1. Church work with gays. 2. Homosexuality–Religious aspects–Christianity. I. Title.
BV4437.5.T56 2004
261.8 ′35766–dc22 2004011974

This book is dedicated to Lenny Carluzzi. Thanks for the hug.

To John Willet, K. D. Kragen, Gary Birkeland, Ben Featheringil, and all the brothers who invited me into their homes and into their lives. Thanks for loving me even when I was certain that there was nothing in me to love.

To my entire family here in Des Moines: Mom, Dad, Jody, and Randy. To my pastors: Tim Rude, Bruce Crane, Mike Bourland, and Nick Ball. To John Drage, Steve Bush, Jeff Kern, and the entire membership of Great Commission Ministries across the world. Thanks for pouring your lives into me!

To Rob Nation: your love and support has been unwavering. To "the Reverend" Matt Roberts: your friendship means more to me than you will ever know. To Brian Petersen, Dave and Steve Rude, Justin and Andrew Meyer, Pete Smith, and all the men of Walnut Creek Community Church: you guys have taught *me* how Jesus would love a homosexual.

To Joseph Nicolosi, Dr. Warren Throckmorton, Richard Cohen, Regina Griggs, Estella Salvatierra, David Pruden, Arthur Goldberg, Joe Dallas, Father John Harvey, Dave Jenkins, Bo and Barb Brink, Kathy Steamer, Linda Delbridge, Kerry Michaelis, Scott Davis, Dick Carpenter, Tim Wilkins, Chuck Wenger, Pavi Thomas, Fred Stoeker, Steve Gottry, Rodney Clapp, Randall Balmer, and Stephen Arterburn for helping me through the publishing process.

And to my God, for bringing all these beautiful people into my life.

For I will give you words
and a wisdom that none of
your opponents will be able to
withstand or contradict.

–Luke 21:15

Contents

Foreword 9

Introduction 11

1. My Story 17
2. Whoever Loves First 31
3. The Homophobia Stops Here 65
4. A God Like Ours 85
5. What Does Science Say? 99
6. What Causes Homosexuality? 111
7. How Does Change Happen? 123

Afterword: Why Can't I Be Proud? 163

Notes 169

Resources 179

FOREWORD

The question "What would Jesus do?" has been repeated, through countless bracelets and bumper stickers, until it has become an unexamined cliché. To the serious believer, of course, what Christ would or would not do is crucial. But when even a crucial thought has been posed too often, it's importance gets watered down. A fresh approach to the same question, then, is needed. And in this vein, the oft asked "What would Jesus do?" could be rephrased and expanded on with another thought: "How would Jesus love?" That's a question Chad Thompson seems to have asked himself, and then, having wrestled with it, he poses it to us as well.

In "Loving Homosexuals as Jesus Would" he asks how we, who claim to be Jesus' followers, can love homosexuals as Jesus loves them? How can we dialogue with them, relate to them, confront them and, in essence, express all that goes with the commandment to walk as Christ walked. Mind you, this isn't an argument coming from a detached philosopher or academic. It comes from a young man who's struggled with homosexuality first hand, and who, like myself and countless others, came to the conclusion that homosexuality falls short of God's intentions.

But just because Chad made the "ex-gay" decision, don't go looking for stereotypical gay bashing in these pages. You'll find, instead, a bold willingness to critique the church's response to lesbian and gay people, along with a call for radical change in the way the Christian community approaches homosexuals and homosexuality. This is, then, a book that will offend some, instruct many, and be relevant to all.

I am especially excited about Chad's efforts in these pages, because I know how difficult it can be trying to capture, then articulate, a balanced, compassionate approach to this issue. Personal demons have to be worked through, terms have to be clarified, a variety of reader's needs have to be considered, and hard truth needs to be balanced with love. So Thompson walks a tightrope here, and invites us to join him as we all seek more effective, biblically based ways to express and defend the faith. God grant that his efforts are rewarded by a deeper understanding and commitment on the part of everyone who reads *Loving Homosexuals as Jesus Would.*

Joe Dallas, author of *Desires in Conflict* and *When Homosexuality Hits Home*

INTRODUCTION

Dr. Rick Warren, pastor of Saddleback Community Church, once said, "There are two basic reasons people don't know Jesus Christ as their Lord and Savior. One, they have never met a Christian. Second, they have met a Christian."

I have written this book because although I am concerned about the claims being made by homosexual groups that insist sexual orientation is unchangeable, I am equally disappointed by the misinformation and malignancy I have seen coming from the Christian church. (For the purposes of this book, when I refer to the church or Christians, I am referring to those who embrace a biblically conservative theology regarding homosexuality.)

While working for a conservative-interest group in Iowa, I was amazed by the high numbers of Christian people who would turn out to oppose homosexuals politically. Yet when I presented opportunities to reach out in love to people who identify as lesbian, gay, bisexual, or transgendered (LGBT), my efforts were often met with apathy and sometimes even hostility. (For the purposes of this book, the terms "LGBT" and "homosexual" will be used interchangeably.)

Not too long ago, I found a comment posted on a Christian website by a gay man that epitomizes the nature of the struggle between the church and the homosexual:

> As a gay male, I do not subscribe to the radical elements of either the right or left. I believe that, as with most politicians, the gay extremists have lost touch with the desires of their so-called constituents.
>
> They have invented an enemy–the religious right–and must perpetuate the imaginary injustices wrought upon them.
>
> I believe that both sides have a radical element which ignores a basic tenet for good living–love thy neighbor.

Many Christians have used the phrase "love the sinner, hate the sin" to describe their attitude toward LGBT people. While there is plenty of evidence that Christians "hate the sin," one must wonder, How does the love manifest itself? How should the love manifest itself?

For Christians to be effective, we must use not only our words but also our hands, feet, minds, hearts, voices, time, resources, and attention to show our love to people who identify as LGBT.

Dr. Vernon Grounds, president emeritus of Denver Seminary, once said, "It seems to me [that showing love] means some *concrete* caring. For example, in the parable of the good Samaritan, it would have been nice to stop and pray for that poor victim who had been beaten up by the robbers. But what about administering whatever first aid you could and alleviating his pain and taking him to a place of safety?" Dr. Grounds then suggested the organization of more police protection for the road, the installation of better lights, and the application of pressure on Jericho's city hall if something was not done to alleviate the traveler's suffering.

For Christians to apply Dr. Ground's suggestion requires that we acknowledge the social and personal struggles faced by LGBT people and that we wage a determined effort to eliminate these struggles, *whether or not they decide to change.*

As much as the church loves to trumpet the stories of men and women who have come out of homosexuality, many in the church have turned a cold shoulder to the needs of those who have embraced their homosexuality, implicitly sending them the message that they must change their sexual orientation in order to become eligible for our love.

The purpose of this book is not to teach Christians how to convince gay people they should change or how to "convert" homosexuals to Christianity. Only God can do these things. The purpose of this book is to teach Christians how to *love* homosexuals, which is our calling (John 13:34). To do this, we must enter the homosexual's world. We must learn to show love in such a way that it can be recognized. In other words, we must "become flesh," just as Christ did for us. Success in doing so requires a humble spirit, a vibrant prayer life, and a thorough understanding of the issues faced by LGBT people.

This book presents a modern-day application of Paul's example in becoming "all things to all people" and explains why an effective ministry to LGBT people who are outside the church requires that we abandon our stereotypes of them and commit ourselves to loving them right where they are.

Furthermore, the church must learn how to love individuals inside the church who have decided to change and are in the process of overcoming homosexual attractions.

There is little question that God's people desire to show love to homosexually oriented people. The roadblock, it seems, is our lack of ability to discern how and when to do so. I was amazed as I listened to the Christian mother of a gay child talk about what she had learned at a Christian conference on homosexuality. She said, "I feel like I have been given permission to love my gay son." While I thought her discovery was wonderful, I had to ask myself, What in the world ever made her think that she *couldn't* love her gay son?

I hope this book will give parents, friends, coworkers, and acquaintances of openly gay and formerly gay people, once and for all, permission to love them without reserve. I also hope this book will show them how to show love. What Pastor Don Richardson believes is "eternity in the hearts of men," Christian author Gary Chapman refers to as the importance of understanding the "love language" of the person you wish to bless. Francis Schaeffer termed it "preevangelism," Paul called it "becoming all things to all people," and John the Baptist described it as "loving first." The concepts described in this book are by no means new; rather, they just have not been applied in ministry to LGBT people. The proper application of these concepts has gotten lost amidst the confusion surrounding the issue of homosexuality.

I did not produce these writings merely to educate individuals who need help understanding this issue or to "tweak" the approach that Christian organizations have taken in homosexual ministry. Rather, these chapters present a call for radical change in the way the evangelical world approaches homosexuals and homosexuality.

Chapters 1 through 3 tell my story and provide solid evidence, biblical and otherwise, for the need to reexamine the way Christians approach homosexuals and homosexuality. In chapter 4, I present a constructive critique of the methods by which religious organizations attempt to combat the biased teaching of homosexuality in America's public schools. Chapter 5 offers a primer on what science has discovered about sexual orientation and examines the research that has been done to find a genetic link to homosexuality.

In chapters 6 and 7, I provide an explanation of the process of changing one's sexual orientation. As someone who is overcoming homosexual attractions, I will describe the process of change and explain how to supplement the transformation of individuals who are redirecting their sexual attractions.

Will God's people persist in turning a cold shoulder to the legitimate struggles of homosexually oriented people, sending them the message that they must change in order to become eligible for our love? Or will we love them *first*? Jesus didn't wait for us to acknowledge *our* sins before filling us up with his love (1 John 4:19).

Neither should we.

I

My Story

For surely I know the plans I have for you, says the Lord, *plans for your welfare and not for harm, to give you a future with hope.*

–Jeremiah 29:11

I'm not gay, I'm not gay, I'm not gay.

When I was twelve years old, I dreamed that I was living in an apartment complex where each of the doors was labeled with the word "fag" instead of the name of the person inside. As soon as I woke up, I analyzed the dream. I concluded that it represented my fear that if people knew I was attracted to men, I would immediately be labeled. I was afraid that because of the label on the outside, no one would want to open the door to find out who I really was on the inside.

Although the dream was unique, the fear I experienced upon realizing I had homosexual feelings was not. I was just one of many young people who begin to wonder how they will survive as homosexuals in a heterosexual world.

I was scared to death.

I'm not gay, I'm not gay, I'm not gay.

I remember the night that I first acknowledged my homosexual attractions. It was the night before my tenth birthday. A cool wind was blowing through the window across from my bed, but there was a tornado in my soul. I could hear the clatter of pots and pans in the kitchen downstairs as my mom baked cupcakes for the next day's celebration. It was so exciting at that age, having a birthday.

I'm not gay, I'm not gay, I'm not gay.

As I lay in bed, my mind spinning in every possible direction as if to eliminate any potential that I may actually fall asleep, I had a breakthrough.

I'm not gay, I'm not gay, I'm not . . .

For some reason, at that moment the denial I had been experiencing since discovering my homosexual attractions–the constant voice in my head that assured me *I'm not gay*–just stopped.

I'm not . . .

I *was.*

I remember the intense seething horror I felt when I realized who, or *what,* I was. I began to think about the things I had heard people say about homosexuals during casual conversation. I was taking an opinion poll in my head. How do people feel about homosexuality? *How will people feel about me?*

As hard as I tried, I couldn't think of a single time that the subject had ever been brought up outside the context of a joke. My mind took me back a few years to a moment at my grandparents' lakeside cabin. Some of my cousins were telling jokes about homosexuals, and I was laughing with them, not even knowing what a homosexual was. But now, I knew. And making the connection between this thing I could tell that people detested and what was going on inside of me was extremely painful, even traumatic.

I heard a symphony of cooking trays playing their tune again as my mom removed the cupcakes from the oven.

Happy birthday to me.

Growing Pains

As time went by, I began to seek information on homosexuality wherever I could find it. I was afraid to check out any books on the subject for fear that my parents would find them. If they did, I'd have some explaining to do. No one could *ever* know about this struggle.

When I turned thirteen, my parents gave me a book about human sexuality. I was so relieved. *Finally*, I thought, *maybe this will explain what's going on inside me.* But all the book said about homosexuality was, "It's very rare; it won't happen to you; don't worry about it."

I was devastated.

In the radio and television messages of the 1980s, I heard the back and forth motion of the culture war swinging like the pendulum on the grandfather clock in my living room. "Gays can change." "No they can't." "Yes they can." "Well, you're homophobic!" I was so confused.

I remember chewing nervously on one of those white foam cups in Sunday school class the morning my teacher taught a lesson on homosexuality. He may have said something about grace or redemption or change. But all I heard him say was, "All homosexuals go to hell," and so I thought I would.

The first time I ever heard anybody say they had changed their sexual orientation was on the *Oprah Winfrey Show*. The audience was skeptical, and so was I.

I would have given *anything* to change. Not primarily because I was worried about what my friends or my family or society would think about me (a fear commonly referred to as "internalized homophobia") but because *I* wanted to change. Not that I didn't care what people would think of me. To the contrary: I was scared to death of being rejected. But I'm just not the conformist type, and my fear of rejection wasn't motivation enough for me to change myself. The desire to change came from within.

Sometime later, I decided to share this struggle with a counselor I had been seeing for clinical depression. It took me two sessions of staring at the floor in silence before I could drum up enough guts to tell him what was going on inside me. Besides the fact that he didn't reject me, which to me was an act of heroism in itself, my counselor explained that homosexuals *can* change. In fact, he had personally counseled many of them through that process.

Wow!

Although the human brain is far too complex to explain homosexual development with a single theory, he told me that, in some cases, men who experience homosexual attractions are, unconsciously, trying to recover their father's love in the arms of another man, and women with homosexual attractions are looking for their mother's love in the arms of another woman. This phenomenon, he explained, is why so many people who experience homosexual attractions report poor relationships with their same-sex parents or peers. The unmet need for love and affirmation from someone of our own gender somehow becomes eroticized when we hit puberty.

This was me growing up. When I reached adolescence, my body started telling me that I wanted sex from a man, but in my heart I knew it wasn't about sex. Even before adolescence, when I used to fantasize about certain men I looked up to and respected, I didn't fantasize about sex. My fantasy was that a man would just wrap his arms around me, look me in the eye, and tell me that I meant something to him.

That's what I was missing.

It wasn't a desire for sex; it was a desire for genuine love and affirmation from someone of my own gender, and I've found that as those needs get met, my homosexual desires fade. In fact, the most healing experience I've had since realizing that I didn't have to be gay was meeting a man named Lenny Carluzzi, who had walked away from homosexuality twenty-eight years ago. Lenny, who has since become my mentor, now lives in Seattle, Washington, with a beautiful wife, two kids, and a dog named Grumpy.

When I first met Lenny at an Italian restaurant in Chicago, he instantly wrapped his arms around me, looked me in the eye, and told me that he loved me. That moment was the beginning of my healing process, and since then God has put dozens of men in my life to provide the nonsexual love and affirmation that I need in order to change. Because of this, I have experienced extraordinary victory over my homosexual desires.

Many books have been written about the process of overcoming homosexual attractions. Scholars have debated, and scientific papers have been published in major scientific journals. But for me, the start of this process was very simple. I just needed to be loved.

That doesn't mean that my homosexual desires are completely gone. Just like anyone trying to change some unwanted trait, such as excess body weight, muscular weakness, or poor academic habits, I have my ups and downs. If I do experience homosexual attractions toward another man, it just means I'm not receiving enough of the *right* kind of love, so I'll call up a male friend for some verbal affirmation or a hug. I think a misconception many people have about those who have changed from homosexual to heterosexual is that we have one cathartic moment we can point to in which every ounce of homosexual desire was drained from our bodies, never to return again. But change takes time.

An important element to the process of change, as I've mentioned, is close, nonsexual relationships with people of one's own gender. I've found, both through my experience and by listening to the stories of others, that anything that creates a sense of disconnection between a child and his or her gender can cause homosexuality. This can manifest itself as rejection, real or perceived, from same-sex parents or peers, or as some form of sexual molestation.

Along these lines, I've found that anything that creates a sense of *reconciliation* between a person and his or her gender can eliminate homosexuality. Two of the most potent ways this can manifest itself is through camaraderie with, and non-sexual touch from, members of one's gender.

I Wanna Hold Your Hand

The first time I experienced the power of touch to combat homosexual desires was the first time I ever met another person who had struggled with those desires. Until that point in my life, most of the hugs I had been given from other men were very short. "Ever straight" men, as my friends and I call them, don't always give the most potent hugs because they fear that if they hold on too long, people might think they're gay. So I had never really been given the kind of hug that I longed for: a long, warm embrace that I could fully internalize as affirmation from another man.

I had just arrived in Chicago for my first-ever meeting with an organization called God Brothers, a support group for homosexual strugglers, and the first thing I did upon exiting the aircraft was run into the arms of a friend named John. We had been talking on the phone for nearly six months about what it would be like to receive a "real hug" from another man.

Before that, I used to roll around in my bed, writhing from the emotional pain that accompanies the deficiency of such an important relational nutrient. At times, my hands would involuntarily grab for inanimate objects in desperation. The only way I can describe this is to say that I was actually experiencing the trauma of emotional pain in my hands. My skin was hungry.

So you can imagine the effect that the arrival of my body in John's arms had on my emotional and physical well-being. It finally put to an end the emotional and physical toll that my adversary, touch-deprivation, was having on me. It was almost ironic, but after years of praying that God would put a man into my life who wasn't afraid to give me a real hug, I now began to pray that God would send someone who would just hold my hand.

That's where Ben came in. He sat next to the couch I was sleeping on during my first night at John's apartment and held my hand until I fell asleep. I remember holding my hands up in the air following that experience and praising God for sending Ben into my life to heal my hands. This healing was miraculous, and though I was too caught up in the drama of meeting so many new people to realize it, I hadn't had a single homosexual thought all weekend.

Another crucial ingredient in my healing process has been camaraderie with my male peers, especially those with whom I can identify. When I see aspects of my personality in other guys my age, it's almost like my masculinity finds a harbor.

I have found that even casual relationships with other guys with whom I can identify create an intense sense of reconciliation between me and my masculinity.

The power of this concept was brought home to me when I went on a three-day pleasure trip to Colorado with two college guys from my church, Justin and Ben. To them, we were just three guys having a good time, but to me, the intensity of the experience was almost overwhelming. Besides the fact that we had an enormous amount of fun during those three days, the constant stream of affirmation from two guys my age with whom I could identify rendered me a complete disgrace to the homosexual orientation. I couldn't have drummed up an erotic attraction to another guy even if I had tried. In fact, the week following the trip, I was inundated with sexual thoughts about men, none of which elicited any chemical or physical reaction in me.

Nonsexual affirmation, when properly internalized, will devour homosexual attractions. But homosexual strugglers require a *constant stream,* not a single dose.

A Dangerous Message?

As I have traveled to speak at high school and college campuses, I have encountered people who call my message "dangerous" and tell me that it's contributing to the suicides of gay youth who need to be accepted for who they are. I understand their concern; I really do.

I can understand how lesbian and gay youth, many of whom are often mocked by their peers and humiliated even by their teachers simply for being different, could view my message as a personal assault. That's why I have never told anyone they *have* to change their sexual orientation in order to be loved by God or by me; I only tell them that they can change if they want to.

A few years ago, I started an organization called Inqueery (www.Inqueery.com) in hopes of opening more doors to tell my story. But Inqueery does not exist to condemn homosexuals who are happy with their sexual orientation. We are merely throwing our hat into the arena of ideas, advocating for a nonbiased discussion of LGBT issues in the public-school setting (see chapter 4). Whether or not students see changing their sexual orientation as beneficial, they at least deserve to know that it can be done.

I have heard the stories of people who, after years or even decades of trying to change their sexual orientation, came up short. These people feel not only as if they put themselves through a torturous process for no reason, but also that they wasted years of their lives. But for many people, the opposite is true. Consider the following comments:

> I wasted fourteen years in therapy with therapists who had a "you're gay, get used to it" mentality–which I find incredibly unethical.

> A lot of people think they are okay being gay. But I never had peace of mind until I started to change.

> I was deceived for a number of years into believing that there was nothing I could do to change my sexual orientation.

> . . . I tried counseling but was simply told to stop fighting the homosexual feelings and accept who I was. I became trapped in the compulsion of cruising, going to the gay bars, and getting involved in a number of empty relationships. . . . The greatest freedom came when I discovered that I could move away from [homosexual behavior] and began to see myself differently.

Why do some people feel as though trying to change was a waste of time and others feel that time was wasted *not* trying to change? For those whose attempts to change seemed unsuccessful, the problem is not that change is impossible but that change is improbable. These individuals likely were given an inaccurate or incomplete explanation of what the process of change entails, or they may have set an unrealistic timeline for their expected transformation. I'll go into more detail about this later. For now, I'll just say that while many factors can add to or subtract from the challenges of going through this process, no one is without the potential to change their sexual orientation. Dr. Joseph Nicolosi, in his book *Reparative Therapy of Male Homosexuality*, writes, "There is always an underlying . . . latent heterosexuality–on which to build change in the client who seeks it."

An accusation I commonly receive during speaking engagements is that my desire to change is not really *my* desire to change. Rather, our homophobic society causes me to want to change so that I can avoid being misunderstood or ridiculed for my homosexuality. But I find this logic hard to swallow because I have been harassed and misunderstood as an ex-gay just as much as I would have been if I had embraced the gay identity. In fact, probably more so. (For the purposes of this book, the term "ex-gay" refers to anyone who has experienced homosexual feelings or behavior and who is in the process of changing his or her orientation.)

Of course, I could avoid all of this hassle by keeping my struggle a secret, which is the solution that Christians usually offer to LGBT people. We say, "Why are homosexuals so blatant, always making a spectacle of their sexuality by kissing in public, wearing wedding rings, and telling everyone what they do in the bedroom?" But asking people to keep themselves a secret is not the solution.

A person's sexuality is not a *huge* deal, but it is a big deal. Forcing someone to hide their sexuality is not healthy because emotional congruency is a central element of mental and spiritual health. Being forced into the closet is not healthy for those who have chosen to embrace their homosexuality, and it's not healthy for those of us who have chosen to come out of homosexuality.

In the same way that ex-gays are often afraid to tell our stories for fear that we'll be ridiculed or even harassed by homosexual activists, some LGBT people live in fear of being ostracized by those who oppose homosexuality on religious or moral grounds. I've heard stories of LGBT people who keep their partners' photographs in their desk drawer at work for fear of being ridiculed by their coworkers, or even terminated by their employer, if their sexuality is discovered.

I believe that loving gay people requires us to fight for their right to live outside the closet without consequence, whether or not we agree with homosexuality. I'll touch on this concept more in the chapters that follow.

2

Whoever Loves First

We love because he first loved us.

—1 John 4:19

I hadn't even arrived at the western Iowa high school where I was scheduled to speak and already I was being attacked. The LGBT student organization at the town's university heard that I was coming, and one of the staff members wrote to the local newspaper, warning people to stay away from my seminar. The day before my visit the group organized a special meeting of students and staff to figure out what they were going to do with me when I got there.

I can't say I wasn't expecting it. I knew that as soon as they read the term "ex-gay" in my seminar description, I would likely walk into that high school carrying the entire history of the Christian church on my shoulders. The anger that was still brewing in their hearts toward every Christian who had ever told them that they were pedophiles or perverts or that they were "going to hell" would be taken out on me. I was "one of those nuts who thinks he changed his sexual orientation" and was going to tell them they all had to do it too in order to qualify for God's love.

Or was I?

The first thing I had to do going into the situation was to figure out what they were expecting me to say so that I could make sure I did not say it. Whatever it was they had heard from the ex-gays who preceded me had obviously not left a good impression.

Some local Christian men who had found out I was coming made it clear that they wanted me to tell the homosexuals that they were all sinners and would go to hell unless they repented of their homosexuality. They also wanted me to warn the homosexuals that their behavior was going to kill them.

I responded by telling these Christian men that although I knew their request was well-intentioned, I felt that doing either of those things would alienate my audience and my entire message would be discounted. I explained that my only purpose was to show love to a group of people who, until my visit, had probably perceived only hatred from those who claimed to represent Jesus.

My hunch was confirmed when one of the men, Raymond, raised his hand at the end of one of the seminars. He told the members of the lesbian and gay group that God loves them, but then he read from Scripture and basically told them they were going to hell. They instantly cut him off.

His ministry was over.

Similarly, I recently received an email from a Christian organization about a seventy-year-old woman who was evicted from her apartment for trying to engage a neighboring tenant, who was gay, in a conversation about hell. She received the eviction notice when this neighbor complained to the apartment manager. The woman said that before this confrontation (which I'm sure was done out of love), she had had a good relationship with her gay neighbor.

She doesn't anymore.

When it came time for me to speak to the students in western Iowa, I think I may have disappointed many of the Christians in attendance by not breaking into a laundry list of the many things that the LGBT students must change about themselves.

Instead, I recounted what it was like for me growing up with homosexual feelings. The pain, the fear, the isolation. Then I launched a PowerPoint presentation that detailed many of the hardships that LGBT people have endured–and I presented solutions. I spoke about the fears involved in "coming out," I spoke against the epidemic of gay epithets, and I touched on the importance of showing respect to LGBT people.

In short, I identified with them.

The fact that I was using words like "discrimination" and "homophobia" threw the Christians in the room for a loop. But the fact that I was saying these things as an ex-gay had the lesbians and gays just as perplexed. I think just about everyone in the room was having a hard time figuring out exactly which side I was on. And the militant homosexual activists who stood at the back with their arms crossed, trying to figure out how they could attack such a respectful, noncondemning message, had looks on their faces that said, "What do we do now?"

Joe Dallas, in his book *A Strong Delusion*, writes about his life before he overcame homosexuality.

> Every day I saw something that reminded me that homosexuality was abnormal, immoral, unequal to heterosexuality. . . . Having struggled so hard to accept my identity, I was not about to reject it again. But the tension between society and me had to be resolved. One of us had to be wrong, and I had already decided it wasn't me. So I needed to convince myself that society erred in its beliefs about, and treatment of, homosexuals.
>
> It wasn't too hard finding evidence to support my belief. Prejudice against gays would crop up occasionally—a "fag" joke overheard in the lunchroom at work, graffiti scrawled on the walls of my favorite gay bar, newspaper accounts of yet another gay man assaulted. All I needed to do was convince myself that prejudice was more than occasional—that it was lurking *everywhere*, lurking behind every negative view of homosexuality, no matter how reasonably that view was

> expressed. Thus *all* objections to homosexuality were, in my mind, born of bigotry or misunderstanding. That made those objections easy to write off as "prejudice," and my comfort with myself would stay intact.

Many lesbian and gay people *need* Christians to be hateful and ignorant in order to convince themselves that our message is the result of ignorance, homophobia, or some massive right-wing conspiracy. But if we take the time to understand them, showing genuine concern for the things that trouble them, they might actually consider our message on its merits. Often LGBT people refuse to accept our message simply because they perceive an ulterior motive on our part. They know that, often, Christians who show them love are doing it only so we can eventually talk them into "going straight." So we must show love to homosexuals regardless of whether they want to change. Real love does not demand anything in return.

Love without Strings

The power of unconditional love was brought home to me when, after my session in western Iowa ended, a gay man named Kevin approached me and asked if I wanted to have lunch with him that afternoon. I'm ashamed to say that initially I doubted his motives. Why was this man, who only minutes earlier had attacked me, calling me "ignorant" and my message "dangerous," inviting me to have lunch with him? Was he going to come on to me? Or worse, try to hurt me?

To the contrary, he wanted to make peace. After completing rounds of personal attacks against me without eliciting so much as a negative tone from my lips, Kevin was left with no legitimate reason to discredit my message. He was forced to analyze my message for what it was, and when he did so, he realized that maybe I had a point.

There are two important ministry concepts at work here. The first one is the importance of presentation. I've found that many LGBT people who are offended by my seminars aren't offended nearly as much by the message that gays can change as they are by the context in which it's given. For the most part, the only time LGBT people ever hear from ex-gays is when our stories of transformation are being used to condemn them. (This is especially true during public-policy debates in which ex-gays' personal testimonies are used as political ammunition to defeat gay civil-rights legislation.)

Kevin later wrote these words in an email to me: "After sitting through your presentation, I was immediately reminded that I needed to be less judgmental of people who self-identify as 'ex-gay,' especially when they, like you, speak out against discrimination and prejudice based on sexual orientation. Until you, I just hadn't met an ex-gay person who was not openly heterosexist and homophobic."

I received a similar email from a young man who had stumbled upon my website while doing some research on gay bashing. He wrote, "If there must be an ex-gay movement out there, I hope you can lead the way. I don't agree with the notion that you can turn somebody into an ex-gay, but I was amazed at the respect you offer homosexuals. Mr. [name omitted] and many other antigay folks could learn from you. Thanks."

The second ministry concept has to do with how we respond to the attacks of those with whom we disagree. Many people respond to the attacks of their adversaries with counterattacks or, at the very least, angry tones and a callous disposition. But these moments of attack are actually the most effective ministry tools we possess. Consider the words of Jesus in Matthew 5: "You have heard that it was said, 'You shall love your neighbor and hate your enemy.' But I say to you, Love your enemies and pray for those who persecute you" (vv. 43–44).

Love is never more potent than when it is given as a response to hatred. Our kindness in such moments will add more to the credibility of our message than the best academic reasoning will ever achieve. Yet, so often, these moments are lost.

During my first "missionary journey" in western Iowa, the LGBT people who attended my seminar leveled their attack against me as soon as I told them that I had changed my sexual orientation. But I remained calm and respectful in my replies, trying to imagine how Jesus would react. But I kept getting interrupted by religious people from the audience who considered arguing to be a more potent response to the LGBT crowd. It didn't seem like love.

A good friend of mine recalls a speech he gave on a college campus a few years ago on the process of change. Toward the end of his message, he was interrupted by a swarm of angry lesbians. These were not your "typical" gay activists. They were loud, violent, and determined to cause trouble. How did my friend respond? He jumped off the platform and, finding himself standing right in front of the leader of this militant mob, asked if he could give her a hug. He said, "You should have seen the look on her face when I asked her that. When I wrapped my arms around her, I could just feel the anger subside as she realized that everything she had assumed about me and my message was wrong. She realized that I really loved her, and a few seconds into the hug, she actually squeezed."

One accusation I seem to hear from religious groups all the time is that LGBT people are not tolerant of those whose views differ from theirs, but that hasn't been my experience at all. The first time I ever spoke on a college campus as an ex-gay, I was verbally attacked by one of the professors in the audience. When the session ended, the president of the college lesbian and gay group actually approached me to apologize for this man's intolerance and to express her acceptance of me as an ex-gay.

Even so, not all homosexuals are tolerant, and even Kevin took some shots at me initially. But I've found that, for the most part, when I present my message in a truly respectful manner, most of the homosexuals who hear it are tolerant. In fact, almost the entire lesbian and gay campus group that had come to my first session in western Iowa to attack me came to my second session, and many of them even supported me.

One of the reasons they accepted my message is that I had the right to give it. Had I gone in there as a straight man and informed them that they were all going to have to change, I would have been eaten alive. But the fact that I actually have changed gives me the right to speak about the possibility of change.

Another reason I was successful is that I did not tell anyone they *had* to change anything about themselves. I've found that if I tell my story in a way that respects the right of others to remain gay, they'll respect my right not to.

Pearls and Swine

Many people would criticize me for not taking a more direct approach. Many would say my approach was flawed because I didn't "tell them the truth" but instead chose to remain morally neutral.

Though there are many biblical accounts in which Jesus chose to be direct with people, usually followed by a run for his life, there are also plenty of accounts in which he didn't. In Luke 20, when the religious leaders ask Jesus by what authority he performs miracles, he actually refuses to tell them, because he knows that he's being led into a rhetorical trap. Later on in the chapter, when he is asked if it's lawful to pay taxes, he responds with a counterquestion.

Jesus showed grace to the humble and disgust with the proud. Much of the time, he spoke to unbelievers in parables they didn't even understand. Jesus had different messages for different people, and so should we. This is what Jesus meant by "casting your pearls before swine" (Matt. 7:6). He was not saying that we should stop communicating God's truth to unbelievers altogether; he was only saying that we should take care in discerning what we teach and to whom we teach it (also see Col. 4:5).

Many Christians, when speaking publicly, are very direct when communicating what they believe the Bible says about homosexuality. When defending their methods, they cite Scripture verses such as Romans 7:7 (which affirms the importance of the law) and Ephesians 5:11 (a command to expose sin). Another passage commonly referenced as a model for evangelism is in Acts 2. Peter boldly proclaims the message of the cross to a group of Jewish people on the Day of Pentecost and then commands them to repent (vv. 22–41). That approach is not always wrong, but it is not always right either.

Most modern evangelism is based on Peter's approach. However, Christian author Ken Ham believes that most modern evangelists have not really considered the methods of evangelism used by the early Christians when speaking to non-Christian audiences. In his book, *Why Won't They Listen?* Ham suggests that Peter was straightforward with the crowd in Acts only because they already understood that they were sinners.

Because the crowd Peter was speaking to was made up of Jews who already had an understanding of the Old Testament, Peter's only job was to convince them that Jesus was the Messiah. Since they already believed in God as the sole creator of the universe, the fall of Adam, and death as the penalty for sin, Peter could come on as strong as he wanted to. Yet in Acts 17, when Paul stands before a crowd that doesn't believe in God, he takes a completely different approach. Instead of demanding they "repent or perish," he actually takes a morally neutral position on idolatry in order to find common ground with them. (I'll discuss this in more detail later.)

The book of Jude also sheds some light on the subject of evangelism. It details two specific but distinct methods of reaching people: "And on some have compassion, making a distinction; but others save with fear, pulling them out of the fire, hating even the garment defiled by the flesh" (vv. 22–23 NKJV). I believe that this particular verse speaks of two separate ways of approaching the gospel: there are times to be bold and speak the truth, and there are times to be gentle and calculated. It is up to us to make the distinction. (Isaiah 28:23–29 uses a farming analogy to illustrate this need for diverse ways to approach ministry.)

Consider Paul's ministry in Corinth. His mission was not to expose the sins of the Gentiles, as this would have only ticked them off and effectively ended his ministry. (Remember Raymond?) Instead, Paul made it his goal to eliminate *anything,* other than the message of the cross, that would offend his audience (1 Cor. 9:12). Paul knew the Holy Spirit would eventually address the sin in their lives (1 Cor. 4:5).

I have been told that trying to "sell the gospel to people without telling them what it's going to cost" is a surefire way to create false converts. But this reasoning is flawed because it assumes that my delivery of the message, rather than the inner working of the Holy Spirit, is responsible for changing hearts. (While human arguments by themselves can accomplish nothing, God does call us to be strategic in the delivery of his message.)

Another problem with the "false convert" ideology is that it sticks God in a box by assuming that he has only one method for calling the lost. God has many ways of reaching people.

While writing this chapter, I received an email from Billy, a member of the LGBT student group in western Iowa who identified with my message and confided in me that he didn't really want to be gay. Now that I've established a dialogue with him, I am free to discuss a variety of topics on a personal basis, including my faith. But he was willing to open up to me only because when we met, I loved him enough to avoid phrasing my message in a way that would offend him.

While many Christians have told me that the only loving way to share the gospel with someone is to "tell them the truth" (point out the sin in their lives), Paul understood that the only truly loving way to share the gospel with someone is to tell them the truth *in such a way that they will respond*. Paul accomplished this by identifying with his mission field. In 1 Corinthians 9, Paul says, "To the Jews I became as a Jew, in order to win Jews. To those under the law I became as one under the law (though I myself am not under the law) so that I might win those under the law. To those outside the law I became as one outside the law (though I am not free from God's law but am under Christ's law) so that I might win those outside the law. To the weak I became weak, so that I might win the weak. I have become all things to all people, that I might by all means save some" (vv. 20–22).

Christian communicator Steve Bush tells the story of a nineteeth-century Chinese missionary:

> Hudson Taylor was a man that went to China 200 years ago to be a missionary, and, as any good British man, he had the ruffles and the long jackets and the knickers and everything. He tried and tried to show these people God's love, but he couldn't get them to understand it because he couldn't get them to understand *him*. So you know what he did? He took off his jacket, he took off his knickers, he took off all of his ruffles and his weird hair, and he grew his hair long and shaved his head bald except for a long ponytail, and he put on the native dress of the Chinese. As soon as the people understood *him*, they were also able to understand his message.
>
> When Hudson went back to his mission organization meeting, he walked in dressed like a native Chinese, and a bunch of the British people almost fell off their chairs. They said, "You've come here and you're acting like one of them!" But to Hudson Taylor that was the whole point.

Sounds like a lot of work. Why go to all the trouble when it's so much easier to shove the Bible in someone's face and call it a day? Because we were *all* initially like the native Chinese, unable to comprehend the message of the cross. It was our inability to understand the Word in the form it had been given to us that created the need for the Word to appear in another form. So the Word became *flesh* (John 1:14). Had it not, none of us would have understood it.

The best way to "become flesh" to people is to identify with them. As I mentioned at the beginning of this chapter, I was able to identify with the LGBT students in western Iowa by recognizing and relating to their hardships. Unfortunately, the church, in general, has been too busy trying to change LGBT people to recognize that some of the discrimination they have faced has truly been unjust. However, most Christians, regardless of how upset we are about the gay political agenda or the indoctrination in the schools, still agree that it's not okay to ridicule homosexuals. So Christians and gays do agree on something! A great way to identify with a person or group is to emphasize common ground.

Eternity in Their Hearts

Paul illustrated the concept of finding common ground with people in Acts 17. While speaking at the Areopagus on Mars Hill in Athens, he quoted pagan philosophers from his era in order to build a bridge to the gospel from concepts the Gentiles already understood. As Paul was reading through pagan writings, he managed to find one paragraph he agreed with, written on an altar to an unknown god. His quoting of this single paragraph established his credibility with the men of Athens and opened up the door for him to share the gospel.

Don Richardson, in his book, *Eternity in Their Hearts*, writes, "Paul could have launched his Mars Hill address simply by calling a spade a spade. He could have said, 'Men of Athens, with all your fine philosophies you still condone idolatry, if not actually practice it! Repent or perish!' And every word might well have been true. . . . But it would have been like a batter hitting the ball and running straight to second base. One must touch first base first!"

Richardson goes on to explain the extent to which Paul is willing to go in order to make a connection with the Gentiles. "Paul 'ran for first' with the following words: 'Men of Athens! I see that in every way you are very religious [remarkable restraint, considering how much Paul loathed idolatry]. For as I walked around and observed your objects of worship [some with Paul's background might have preferred to call them "filthy idols"], I even found an altar with this inscription: TO AN UNKNOWN GOD.'" Paul then went on to explain to them that their "unknown god" is the one true God and eventually transitioned to the message of the cross. Paul wanted so much to win the Gentiles over that he was willing to present a morally neutral position on idolatry in order to find common ground with them.

Jesus sought common ground with the Sadducees. Because the Sadducees considered only Genesis through Deuteronomy to be inspired, Jesus referenced these writings when addressing them. Jesus also sought common ground with the woman at the well in John 4. He could have started a conversation with her about any number of topics, but since drawing water from the well was her responsibility, Jesus got her attention when he offered her water that would cause her never to thirst again (v. 14).

Many Christian churches find common ground with young people by sponsoring concerts with Christian punk bands. When the concert is over, the youth pastor can present the gospel and the teenage audience will actually listen. Churches that send missionaries overseas or start outreach programs in international cities find common ground with foreigners by studying the language and culture of the people they are trying to reach. But have Christians found our common ground with the lesbian and gay community?

Unfortunately, I believe that few Christians have found common ground with LGBT people. Most of the time when I hear Christians speak on homosexuality, they focus on the "myth" that homosexuals make up 10 percent of the population or they attack the credibility of estimates of the gay suicide rate. One Christian group's website has a section called "homosexual urban legends," which is nothing more than a laundry list of every issue that has caused contention between the homosexual community and the church.

Not long ago, I picked up a gay-published "resource guide" about homosexuality. I was particularly interested to find out exactly what it said because similar books had been severely criticized by many prominent conservative-interest groups. Many of the things I read in it were the same things I have written about in this book, things I agree with. There were really only a few things with which I had a major problem; namely, the claim that sexual orientation cannot be changed and that trying to do so is "dangerous."

So I decided that Inqueery would publish our own resource guide, including many of the things that are in the gay version, minus those parts that claimed that sexual orientation cannot be changed. Even though I disagreed with a few of the things in the homosexual booklet, I chose to emphasize the things I did agree with, and because I did, the message that gays can change is being heard by people who normally would not even give an ex-gay the time of day.

In virtually all of Inqueery's publications, we emphasize those issues on which we agree with the LGBT community. Our resource guide has a section that explains why we feel it's important that homosexuality is addressed in the public schools (see chapter 4). Obviously Inqueery presents a different message than most homosexuals do, but the fact that we agree that the subject should be talked about in the schools at all is significant. Inqueery's resource guide also has sections designed to help straight people overcome common stereotypes of LGBT people.

As important as knowing what to say when speaking to those with whom we disagree is knowing what not to say. It wasn't by accident that Paul's message on Mars Hill differed from messages he had given to other people groups. Instead of reciting straight from the Bible or reciting Jewish history as he normally did, Paul took the approach he did with the Gentiles because he had disciplined himself to tailor his message to the perspective of his audience.

Paul was not addressing a typical audience here. The Mars Hill Society was a group of prominent Athenians that met on Mars Hill to discuss philosophy, history, and religion. Don Richardson writes, "Paul's success in the main part of his address would depend upon one thing. Call it 'gapless logic.' As long as each successive statement which Paul made followed logically from statements preceding, the philosophers would listen. . . . It was a rule of the philosophical training they had received."

Making a Distinction

Proper application of Paul's mission strategy requires that we conduct our dialogue in a way that is sensitive to how LGBT people view their condition. In other words, we must be aware of the "philosophical training" LGBT people have received from the secular voices of our society.

Often when Christians attempt to discuss certain issues with LGBT people, communication breaks down because the two sides are basing their arguments on differing assumptions about homosexuality. Many Christians view homosexuality as a behavior that can be altered, but most homosexuals view it as an immutable identity.

To many Christians, it makes perfect sense that lesbians and gays should not be granted civil-rights protection. We say, "It's common sense that a chosen behavior does not constitute grounds for special protection." But to LGBTs, who likely do not believe their condition can be altered, civil-rights protection is a logical request. They say, "It's common sense that protection should be granted based on an immutable identity." This is a great example of the distinction mentioned in Jude 22. If Christians consider homosexuality a behavior, but homosexuals consider it an identity, is it really possible to hate the sin without also hating the sinner?

Not in their eyes.

Making this distinction will help us determine which of the two ministry approaches mentioned in Jude we should take: blatant proclamation against behaviors considered sinful or compassionate outreach. Bear in mind, I'm not suggesting that we cannot maintain a balance of the two, but this verse in Jude is saying that in some situations, it's best to choose one over another.

In at least two Christian books, I've seen the phrase "coming out" defined as the process of "revealing perverse sexual practices to family and friends." Again, since LGBT people view their condition as an identity, rather than a behavior, using terminology like this will serve only to alienate us from them, possibly eliminating any potential for ministry. (Furthermore, not everyone who identifies as LGBT has participated in the sexual behaviors associated with homosexuality.)

A better response would be to recognize that many people who struggle with their sexual orientation, whether gay or ex-gay, are scared to death that they'll be rejected by their friends and family if they disclose this struggle. I know I was.

Randy Newman of Campus Crusade for Christ tells the story of a young man named Jim who was struggling with homosexuality. Jim was debating whether he should tell members of his campus fellowship about his struggle, but when another student in the group requested prayer for his gay roommate, the group's director condemned homosexuality instead of offering prayer for the roommate. "Jim told us he decided, then and there, that this was not a safe place to talk about his homosexuality."

When discussing the subject of homosexuality, we should use words that reveal our genuine concern for those who are struggling with their sexual identity. This will send the message to those around us that it is safe for them to talk to us about their sexuality, that it is safe for them to "come out" to us. This means using words that are inclusive, not divisive. While homosexuals use words like "love" and "relationship" to describe homosexuality, Christians use words like "sin" and "abomination." When addressing our lesbian and gay neighbors, we must put aside language that we know will alienate them.

From the homosexual's perspective, many of the phrases that Christians throw around sound completely absurd. Applying these phrases to heterosexuality might help us to understand their frustration.

- What do you think caused your heterosexuality?
- When and how did you first decide you were heterosexual?
- Is it possible that heterosexuality is a phase you will grow out of?
- To whom have you disclosed your heterosexuality? How did they react?
- Heterosexuality isn't offensive as long as you leave others alone. Why, however, do so many heterosexuals try to seduce others into their orientation?
- Many child molesters are heterosexuals. Do you consider it safe to expose your children to heterosexuals? Heterosexual teachers particularly?

- Why are heterosexuals so blatant, always making a spectacle of their heterosexuality? Why can't they just be who they are and not flaunt their sexuality by kissing in public, wearing wedding rings, and so on?
- Given the problems heterosexuals face, would you want your children to be heterosexual? Would you consider reparative therapy to try to change them?

It's important to note that I'm not implying these are legitimate questions or that homosexuality is on par with heterosexuality. I also am not saying we should compromise what we know to be true in order to avoid angering someone who is homosexual. Some people will be angry at us no matter how we present our message. I am only suggesting that, whenever possible, we should avoid using terminology that will offend homosexuals.

The bottom line is, if we really want to enter the homosexual's world–become flesh, if you will–we must embrace a new way of communicating with them. Instead of looking at them through the world's eyes, *we need to look at the world through their eyes.*

Ken Ham writes, "As I have traveled around other parts of the world, mixing with different cultures, I have increasingly come to realize how important it is to understand how people think, *before* trying to communicate with them." Understanding how people think will allow us to frame our message in such a way that they will respond. This will also help us avoid using terminology that will hinder our outreach. The ability to do this successfully requires that we abandon common misconceptions about homosexuals and homosexuality.

One common misconception about LGBT people is that they are all pedophiles. Yes, some research has suggested that, by population, a higher percentage of homosexuals than heterosexuals molest children. But *by far* the majority of homosexuals are not pedophiles. Even Dr. Jeffrey Satinover, author of perhaps the most well-known conservative book on the subject of homosexuality, writes, "It is true that pedophilia is more common among homosexuals than heterosexuals–and vastly more common among males, heterosexual or homosexual, than among females. But it is also true that the majority of homosexuals are not pedophiles."

My favorite misconception is that homosexuality is something people "choose." It gets repeated on Christian radio programs and TV shows all the time, and it's all I can do not to laugh out loud when I hear it because it's so absurd! Homosexual *behavior* is, obviously, something people must choose to engage in, just as heterosexual behavior is, but neither homosexual nor heterosexual *orientation* is initially a choice. I often confuse people when I say that a homosexual orientation is not a choice, because they've heard me say that there's no gay gene (see chapter 5). If there isn't a gay gene, it must be a choice. Right?

Wrong.

Homosexual attractions are not genetic or chosen; rather, they are *developed* during childhood, usually in response to a lack of affirmation from and identification with one's own gender. Because this process is unconscious, it's not fair to say that lesbian and gay people "choose" to be that way.

A New Strain of Leprosy

Another common misconception among religious people is that homosexuals are solely responsible for the AIDS epidemic. While no one can deny that homosexuality has played a profound role in the spread of AIDS, research has found that heterosexual promiscuity, as well as intravenous drug use, also contribute to the spread of AIDS in the United States.

Many of the people living in third-world countries like Africa who have been stricken with AIDS probably don't even know what the phrase "sexual orientation" means. Yet some Christians insist that AIDS is God's judgment on LGBT people. It's not. (However, it should not be ignored that AIDS is still a major risk factor for people who are sexually promiscuous, gay or straight.)

I think few Christians have an accurate picture of the pain that the AIDS epidemic has caused, and many don't want an accurate picture. Some time ago a church I used to attend invited a mother whose son died of AIDS to speak to the congregation, but they refused to let her display photographs of her son's final year on their big screen. The pictures, though grotesque and discomforting, could have served as a valuable tool for motivating that church body to get involved in AIDS ministry, but the church dropped the ball in order to preserve the comfort of its members.

Jerry Arterburn is a Christian man who died of AIDS as a result of homosexuality. In his book *How Will I Tell My Mother?* Jerry writes about his experience visiting a fellow AIDS patient:

> His arms and legs were no larger around than quarters. He lay there on his back with his bony knees brought up to his chest in a fetal position. He didn't have a hair on his head; it had all fallen out from therapy. He was a prisoner of the disease, and he looked as if he had just been released from a cruel prisoner-of-war camp. He was shocked that anyone had come in, especially a stranger like me. He asked me in a soft but startled voice, "Who are you?" I told him I was Jerry and asked him who he was. He told me his name was Ron. I told him that I was an AIDS patient who was being treated on an outpatient basis and that I had stopped in to say hi. He broke into tears as he told me that it had been about five weeks since anyone had come to see him. His loneliness and isolation caused me to cry. He was part of a deserted group of people who are being treated like the lepers described in the Bible.

So often we hear AIDS patients and other cultural "undesirables" compared to the lepers of Jesus' time, and while this analogy may solicit some compassion for such socially starving people, I wonder how many people really understand just how bad it was for the lepers.

In his book *The Jesus I Never Knew*, Philip Yancey draws attention to the inhumanities faced by those with leprosy. People in Jesus' day held the belief that all disease was the result of sin, therefore few had any compassion for those who were afflicted with such a disease. Levitical laws required lepers to live outside city walls and yell "Unclean!" when they approached anyone. Furthermore, all lepers had to wear the clothes of a mourner going to a burial service and keep at least a six-foot distance from everyone else. Getting too close to a leper would make a person "unclean" according to the laws of Moses, and touching a leper was just unheard of.

You can imagine the emotional toll this must have taken on those who were unlucky enough to be diagnosed with the disease. Yancey tells this story of Dr. Paul Brand, a modern-day leprosy specialist, who was treating a young man in India who had leprosy: "In the course of the examination Brand laid his hand on the patient's shoulder and informed him through a translator of the treatment that lay ahead. To his surprise the man began to shake with muffled sobs. 'Have I said something wrong?' Brand asked his translator. She quizzed the patient in a spurt of Tamil and reported, 'No, doctor. He says he is crying because you put your hand around his shoulder. Until he came here no one had touched him for many years.'"

Back in Jesus' day, and today as well, people with leprosy are damaged far more by the isolation and rejection that accompany their malady than by the disease itself. As Mother Teresa said, "We have drugs for people with diseases like leprosy. But these drugs do not treat the main problem of being *unwanted*."

Millions of people, gay and straight, are lying in hospitals all around the world waiting to die from the AIDS virus. Some of them, but especially those who are lesbian or gay, have been rejected by their families and are suffering alone. *Unwanted.* Because they know their time is short, they are usually very open to spiritual matters, but there is seldom anyone around to talk to them about it. Jerry Arterburn concluded his earlier quote with these two questions: *"Where are the local churches? Why aren't they coming to minister to these people?"*

While there are a few excellent Christian groups involved in ministry to AIDS patients (see the resources section), the majority of the resources available for people living with AIDS and HIV are from homosexual organizations. There have been many opportunities to minister to people with HIV and AIDS, yet because most churches have chosen not to get involved, someone else has loved them first.

If You Can't Say Something Nice . . .

Besides avoiding popular myths about homosexuality, we must also avoid using outdated or divisive terminology, such as calling homosexuals "sodomites," or calling homosexuality a "lifestyle," which implies that there is one lifestyle that all gays adhere to, instead of realizing that, like straight people, LGBT people represent a variety of different lifestyles.

It's true that some may get stone drunk each night and then take some stranger home for sex, the stereotype that many Christians have of gay people, but others could be your neighbors, your relatives, even your children. It is also true that research has found promiscuity to be prevalent among homosexuals and that some gay relationships involve grotesque physical distortions and anonymous sexual contacts. But Christians often discount the potential of LGBT people to enter into relationships that consist of genuine love.

Many studies claim to prove that fidelity among homosexual partnerships is virtually nonexistent. One study says that the average lifespan of a homosexual is forty-two years; another study says 43 percent of male homosexuals reported having more than five hundred partners during their lifetime.

For the purposes of this book, I won't take the time to dissect the research methods used to draw these conclusions. I will only say that while some of the findings in such studies are true, throwing these numbers around while talking to LGBT people will only reinforce, in their minds, the fact that you have stereotyped them. Can you imagine telling your son or daughter that heterosexuality is inherently evil because America has a divorce rate estimated at 43 percent or because 30 percent of women killed in the United States die at the hands of a husband or boyfriend?

A better way to engage in a conversation with someone who is lesbian or gay is to talk about the things that interest you or to find out what interests them. Oftentimes when Christians speak to LGBT people, we get so caught up with the fact that they are gay that we find it nearly impossible to transition to any other subject. Talk about family, work, school, politics . . . even the weather if you must! Homosexuality is only one aspect of an LGBT person's life.

A proper understanding of sexual development, the abandonment of homosexual myths, and the avoidance of divisive terminology are all necessary if we desire any kind of ministry with LGBT people. And of course, the most potent ingredient in effective ministry is the ability to love successfully. As Christians, we can be as well-intentioned as we want to be, but if our approach alienates those we are trying to love, it may be time to try something else.

Gary Chapman, in his book *The Five Love Languages*, writes, "We must be willing to learn our spouse's primary love language if we are to be effective communicators of love." Although Chapman wrote his book to help strengthen marriages, I believe this concept can be applied universally. So what does love look like to someone who is lesbian or gay? We cannot know the answer if we do not know someone who is lesbian or gay. If we really want to enter their world–become flesh–we must learn to see life through their eyes. Doing so will allow us to frame our *love* to them in such a way that they will understand. So how, specifically, should one go about this?

- There is something profoundly genuine about being invited into someone's home for a meal. Anyone can attend a rally or pass out a tract, but inviting someone into your home is so deeply personal that it will be hard for anyone to discount your sincerity.

- Attend a gay-pride rally in your city, not to politically demonstrate against homosexuals but simply to build relationships with them. For the past few years, I have attended the gay-pride parade in Des Moines simply to pass out cold water and pizza to the lesbian and gay people in attendance.
- Assemble a group from your church who is willing to make a trip to the local hospital at least once a month to comfort AIDS patients. This does not have to be a big production; just take them a can of pop or some soup, ask them how they are doing, and then let them know how much God loves them. (You may have to undergo volunteer training through the hospital before gaining admittance.)
- If you know someone who is dying of AIDS, offer financial assistance, since unemployment is the eventual consequence of AIDS. HIV and AIDS patients, especially those who don't have insurance, are often overburdened by a decrease in income and an increase in medical bills.
- Invite a homosexual, or someone who is working to overcome homosexuality, from within your church to a Bible study group or other social event. For people who struggle with homosexuality, getting connected to others can prove very difficult, especially when it comes to one's same-gender peers. (I'll discuss this more in chapter 7.)

- Invite a homosexual person from *outside* of your church to your Bible study or other social event. Often homosexuals don't attend church because they fear rejection from Christians, whom they believe would never accept them. A simple invitation can make a world of difference.
- Ask your church to sponsor a forum on homosexuality. Invite an ex-gay who is willing to share his or her testimony in a humble and compassionate manner. You can advertise the forum in the local newspaper and even recruit students to pass out flyers in the public school. When gay students and other members of the homosexual community show up, seize the opportunity to show interest in their lives. (Warning: there are a few public figures in the ex-gay community who claim to be compassionate but actually just want to preach at or condemn homosexuals. Be very careful about whom you choose to speak at your event.)
- Sometimes listening can be even more important than speaking. If you host a forum on homosexuality, invite someone from the gay community to share some of the struggles faced by lesbian and gay people in your town. This is their chance to show you how to love them, and remember, no strings attached. You are not trying to change them; you only want to love them.
- Set up a mentoring program in your church by holding training sessions for heterosexual men and women who want to better understand and help struggling homosexuals. (You could use this book as the curricu-

> lum.) Then pair the heterosexual men and women with the homosexually struggling men and women. Some churches, such as Emmanuel Reformed Church in Paramount, California, have done this in an effort to provide a mentoring relationship for homosexual strugglers who may otherwise have a hard time connecting with their same-gender peers.

Members of the Church of the Open Door in San Rafael, California, have come up with a few other suggestions for befriending homosexual strugglers within their congregation, such as sending them a birthday card, phoning them periodically to offer encouragement, including them on a family outing, and having them bring a potluck item to your house for a holiday meal. In addition, if you have been praying for specific people, let them know you are praying for them. This can be far more powerful than you might think. It's also a great way to start a spiritual conversation with an unbeliever.

Lenny Carluzzi talks about his experience ministering to a man who decided to leave behind his homosexuality:

> Having just lost his lover of seven years, I knew that if I merely dropped Randy off at church and told him to meet people he would surely die on the vine. So our family became the loving hands of Christ extended to him. Randy spent countless hours over at our house, so much so that he became known as "Uncle Randy" to our kids. He participated in all of the

activities that made up our family functions and holidays, including doing dishes and taking out the trash!

Of course we all enjoyed worshiping together in church, and studying the Bible in Sunday school, but it was the day to day love we gave Randy that gave him the confidence he needed to succeed in his new life.

It's been twelve years since Randy made the decision to walk away from homosexuality, and he is now married to a lovely woman and has two sons.

Often when I've attended political events, either pro-gay or anti-gay, I have seen Christian men debating LGBT people on a variety of issues and ideas. While these ideas certainly are of paramount importance to our lives and our world, when standing alone, they lack the power to change lives.

I once heard a pastor on the radio say that he has never heard someone say in their testimony, "You know, I lost an argument and so I just yielded myself to Christ." Instead, from those who have been wooed into God's kingdom, we hear talk about the gentleness of the person who ministered to them and the love that captured them.

There's no doubt that the mind plays a role in salvation (1 Peter 3:15), so we must introduce our ideas. But whose ideas will make the cut? To whom will a person who is unsure what to do with their discovery of same-sex attractions go for help? To the homosexual community, which not only provides acceptance but also genuinely understands the issues gay people face, or to the church, whose claim to love

LGBT people has too seldom made it outside the doors of our sanctuaries?

While the church and the homosexual will always disagree on ideas, we must realize that the battle we fight, ultimately, is not for the cessation of gay curriculum in public schools, the validity of orientational change, or even the credibility of the latest gene research. Rather, the battle we fight is a battle for the hearts of our world's LGBT people.

And whoever loves first, wins.

3

The Homophobia Stops Here

There is no fear in love, but perfect love casts out fear.

—1 John 4:18

As our hands met in greeting each other, I tried to make eye contact with Phillip, but he would not look at me. The handshake was just a formality, and eye contact certainly was not necessary. After all, he thought I was there only to announce God's judgment on him and his lesbian and gay friends, just as so many evangelicals before me had. I would probably start by telling him that he "chose" to be gay, the misconception for which Christians are famous. Then I would tell him that he must go straight to be eligible for God's love, and I would most likely end the conversation with some lame cliche like "love the sinner, hate the sin."

Or would I?

Phillip and others like him know too well the attitude of many Christians. He has heard the derogatory tones coming from the pulpit and the barbs of inflammatory humor about gays that sneak into daily conversation. These things serve as evidence that homophobia is alive and well, even in the church.

Some individuals may crack inappropriate jokes about LGBT people simply because they are insensitive. However, I believe that some of the ridicule aimed at LGBT people is coming from insecure men who are trying to prove that they are heterosexual by ridiculing those who aren't.

In his book, *Healing the Masculine Soul*, Gordon Dalbey writes, "Homosexuals are quick to charge their critics with 'homophobia'–and in fact, they are largely justified in doing so. For the vast majority of us males in our father-starved culture justly fear a misfocused attraction to other men."

Say It Loud!

Conservative groups and ex-gay ministries have put much effort into educating churches about the need for ministry to LGBT people, and progress *is* being made. But some of that progress, I fear, is only rhetorical.

As Christians, we've learned to say we love LGBT people, but how does that love manifest itself? Do we really love homosexuals, or do we just say we love them while inwardly gagging in disgust?

A good friend of mine who has overcome homosexuality offered some classes on homosexuality in his church. Keenly aware of the anxiety in the room, he opened his talk by asking everyone to face their fears by saying the word "homosexual" out loud. He describes what followed: "Muted mumbles simultaneously rippled about the room, some faces turned red in embarrassment, some people repositioned their seats while others just cleared their throats or laughed nervously."

I can see the change in body language when I talk to some of my "ever straight" friends about my past and the fact that I still occasionally experience attractions to men. They fold their arms over their chests and look down as if to say, "Let's not talk about this anymore."

Some time ago, I heard the story of a missionary who was struggling with homosexuality. For quite a while, he lived in fear that someone would find out about this struggle, but after he finally drummed up enough guts to disclose it to a Christian friend whom he had known for thirteen years, his friend wouldn't even ride in a car with him for fear of being seen with a homosexual. I've heard stories of Christian men refusing even to shake hands with someone who disclosed a struggle with homosexual feelings.

That's homophobia.

Some criticize me for using the word "homophobia" in my materials because it's "their" word. I've been told that gay activists made it up for the sole purpose of attacking Christians who oppose homosexuality. There's no doubt that the word has been used to condemn Christians, but actually it was coined in the late 1960s by a heterosexual man. Psychologist George Weinberg came up with the term to describe heterosexuals' dread of being in close quarters with homosexuals. Regardless of the motivation behind the use of the term, Christians should recognize that there is truth behind its meaning. (Even Paul was known to quote secular phrases that contained truth as a way of connecting to his audience; see 1 Cor. 6:12–13.)

People versus Politics

While I can't help but disagree with some of the characterizations LGBT people sometimes make about Christians, I must consider that to some extent, we asked for it. For the better part of America's history, few churches addressed the issue of homosexuality at all. Nobody really understood what it was or why it happened, and most people didn't want to.

In 1976, a markedly successful crusade to repeal a gay-rights measure that had been passed in Dade County, Florida, was initiated by a former celebrity named Anita Bryant. Bryant's activism spearheaded an astounding response from religious leaders, most notably televangelists, who understood the Florida legislation only as an endorsement of sin. Many malignantly characterized LGBT people as child molesters and rallied relentlessly for the defeat of their political endeavors, but few offered redemption. Scores of hurting and confused people were condemned, while the emotional and spiritual ramifications of their sexuality were left to them to resolve. This situation created a sure supply of political ammunition for the homosexual political leaders of my generation, and a community of people who spoke so incessantly about "loving the sinner," missed the opportunity of a lifetime to minister to these hurting people.

Referring to the AIDS epidemic of the 1980s, Joe Dallas writes, "Where were [the church's] missions, our visitation programs, our calls to action? . . . While we pointed our fingers, the non-believers and the cults extended their hands." While I'm sure there were some Christians responding with compassion to the needs of LGBT people, the most prominent spokespersons for the evangelical church at that time spoke of AIDS only when referring to God's wrath on the "sodomites of America." For this, we owe an apology.

Today, one of the most prevalent causes of Christian mischaracterizations of LGBT people is the inability to separate gay people from gay politics. It's true that many gay political groups are up to no good. They are implementing biased public-school programs, passing legislation that could make it illegal for Christians to quote passages of Scripture that discuss homosexuality, and even trying to outlaw therapy for those who wish to change from gay to straight.

As we become familiar with the goals of the militant side of the gay political movement, it's natural that we should become angered, even disgusted, by their attempts to invade our courtrooms and indoctrinate our children. However, if we lack the ability to separate an individual from the goals of these political groups, we might as well point all African Americans to the back of the bus because we disagree with the philosophies of a certain African American special interest group. (Important: I am not comparing sexual orientation to skin color; I am merely trying to illustrate how absurd it is to define an entire demographic by the interest groups that claim to represent it.)

For many people, the only thing that comes to mind when they hear the word "homosexual" is the militant gay activist marching in a parade and shouting, "We're here, we're queer, and we're coming after your children!" One prominent Christian organization has a picture on its website of a homosexual man scowling at a little boy as if he's about to harm him. The man's face has been tinted green as if to suggest that he is a demon.

When I was in charge of writing the newsletter for a Christian special interest group, I included a story whose content was similar to that of this chapter. The message of the article, in summary, was, "homosexuals are people too." But this concept was too much for my readership. Three of the newsletters were sent back to me, something that had never happened before. Two of them had writing scribbled on the front that said things like, "You are deluded!" and, "Remember Sodom and Gomorrah!" The third one demanded that we take them off of our mailing list immediately to avoid legal action.

I wish I could say this attitude is limited to three people on the mailing list of the organization I used to work for, but I have found that it is much more widespread. I received an email at work from a woman who clearly had made her mind up that all homosexuals are exactly the same:

> I became very well informed of the homosexual agenda. . . . *Their* leaders then stated that we . . . could have our churches and our schools but that *they* were coming for our boys. Yes! Thus I have no compassion for *that crowd*. . . . Did you know *they* kill each other in jealous rages [sic]. *They* also infect each other and female marriage partners with AIDS and sexually transmitted diseases. . . . There are homosexuals who stay married to their wives. *They* are not the good "boys" on the block [emphasis added].

Yes, some homosexuals do molest children, and there are many homosexual political groups whose goals are intrinsically evil. But we must keep in mind one important truth: their membership is limited.

This concept was first brought home to me when I met a young man named Jerynn Johnston. He appeared on television, and was written about in newspapers all across the state when he fought to get the words "sexual orientation" added to his high school's nondiscrimination policy. I'm sure many who read his story viewed it as a determined effort to advance some massive homosexual agenda thought up by a well-funded homosexual advocacy group in Washington, D.C. However, during a conversation I had with Jerynn, I casually mentioned the homosexual political group at the national forefront of the issue he was battling, and he hadn't even heard of it. Jerynn is just a high-school kid who is sick of getting his tires slashed because he's gay.

Please understand, I do not underestimate the influence of the many homosexual advocacy groups in existence today.

They are large and they are powerful. I'm only pointing out that not all LGBT people agree with their goals and their motives.

Conservative-Interest Groups

I believe that irresponsible conservative-interest groups are another factor contributing to the mischaracterization of LGBT people. Stereotypes of LGBT people are reinforced when conservative-interest groups, in order to scare people into sending them money, call attention to fringe movements within the gay community that are especially militant. In the book *Blinded by Might*, Cal Thomas, speaking against this practice, writes, "One must constantly have enemies, conspiracies, and opponents as well as play the role of righteous victim in order to get people to send in money."

I find it very disappointing when I receive emails from a certain conservative-interest group that contain a photograph of a gay teacher holding a picket sign. The email includes a request for money so this group can "combat the gay agenda in the public schools." Don't send money to groups who claim to be combating the homosexual political agenda in public schools, or anywhere else for that matter, unless they tell you specifically how they plan on doing it.

Furthermore, when I consider that most of the conservative-interest groups that deal with homosexuality are run by Christian people, it surprises me how quiet they remain when LGBT people are attacked by radicals like Fred Phelps. Phelps, who currently serves as pastor of Westboro Baptist

Church in Topeka, Kansas, has conducted over 20,000 sidewalk demonstrations using picket signs that say things like "THANK GOD FOR AIDS," and "GOD HATES FAGS." When Phelps was in Iowa, I attended a counter-protest led by a local gay-advocacy group. As I sang along with the protest organizers' rendition of "We Shall Overcome," my eyes wandered about the rotunda of the Iowa State Capitol looking for my Christian friends. But they never showed up. It occurred to me afterward that had the purpose of Phelps's visit been to condone homosexual behavior, Iowa's major conservative-interest groups would have led Christians there in droves to oppose Phelps's misrepresentation of the Scriptures. But isn't the claim that God hates homosexuals a misrepresentation as well?

By claiming that God hates lesbian and gay people, Phelps is contributing to an atmosphere of hatred, ridicule, and violence. While the majority of people will see through his rhetoric, the small number that takes such sentiments to heart is enough to make our world a dangerous place for LGBT people. If you don't believe this, ask Judy Shepard. Her son Matt was tied to a fencepost, beaten, and left for dead. Many believe that this happened because he was gay.

Despite the potential consequences of Phelps's message, most of those who oppose homosexuality chose not to take a public stand against him when he was in Iowa, fearful that opposing Phelps and his ilk was tantamount to condoning the lifestyles of lesbians and gays.

While I do commend the conservative groups that have issued press releases condemning Phelps's hypocrisy, we need to work harder at balancing our activism against the homosexuals' political agenda with activism against those who unjustly condemn gays. I would also like to see the leaders of ex-gay ministries take a more proactive role in fighting homophobia directed toward openly lesbian and gay people. I have often wondered, as I watch the pain and ridicule that so many LGBT people experience, why everyone who comes out of homosexuality so quickly forgets how painful this is. How is it possible that their message so abruptly jumps from one that combats the unjust discrimination and name calling of homosexual people to a decidedly narrow focus on the need to change?

Ten Phobias

Homophobia is an especially dangerous threat to the kingdom of God not only because it shortens the arms of Christ to reach those who embrace a gay identity but also because it stifles the progress of those who are overcoming homosexual attractions. As far as the church is concerned, promises of hope and healing sometimes translate into uncomfortable looks or polite smiles from people who, truth be told, are disgusted that a member of their church has been involved in "that lifestyle." That's homophobia.

It's important to note, however, that the church has made astounding progress in the past few years. Most of the people in my church have reacted positively to the addition of an ex-gay person to our congregation.

Lenny Carluzzi writes about ten fears that represent the different facets of homophobia in the church. The first four phobias apply to those who are in the process of overcoming homosexual attractions:

1. Inherency: Christian people who struggle with a homosexual orientation fear that their condition is, as they've heard from the media, inborn.

   What if all these psychological theories that Christians perpetuate on how to change from gay to straight are bogus? What if all these "ex-gays" are just faking it? What if it really is inborn?
2. Identity: Sometimes it is other Christians who doubt that anyone can really change; in doing so, they put the blood of Christ on trial.

   What if I will always be viewed by other church members as a homosexual? What if people are afraid to get close to me or continue to judge me because of my past?
3. Inadequacy: Men and women who have struggled with homosexual orientations often have a hard time relating to members of their gender. In some cases, this is because they were rejected by them during the formative years of their lives, a factor that many psychologists believe contributes to the development of a homosexual orientation (see chapter 6).

   What if I can't relate to heterosexual men? What if they get together to watch sports and they can tell I don't find it interesting? What if I get nervous when I'm around them and make a fool of myself? (It's important to note that these thoughts do not apply to all men who struggle with homosexuality. I have one ex-gay friend who lives and breathes football; he's even a sports reporter for a newspaper!)

4. Incompatibility: Homosexual strugglers often question their capability to function in a heterosexual manner.

   What if we get in the bedroom and I make a fool of myself? What if I am not able to fulfill a woman emotionally or sexually in the context of marriage? (Interesting to note that these fears can apply to heterosexual men as well!)

The next six phobias apply to heterosexual Christians who may have the opportunity to minister to a homosexual struggler:

5. Infatuation: Many heterosexual men simply fear that some "gay guy" is going to fall in love with them. Part of this fear may come from some insecurity in their masculinity, and part of it may come from their reluctance to be depended on.

   If I befriend an ex-gay, he will develop a crush on me or demand more time than I am willing to give. What if he falls in love with me? How do I know if he likes me for who I am, or if he's only hanging out with me because he's attracted to me? If I befriend him, will he make a move on me?

6. Influence: Many people are still under the impression that all homosexuals are pedophiles or that homosexuality is something you can "catch." Therefore, people who have never struggled with homosexuality

are sometimes afraid to spend time with individuals who have a homosexual past.

If we share a room at this conference, will I have to sleep in the same bed with him? What if he comes on to me during the night? He can't come over to my house; what if he molests my kids? (I have one ex-gay friend who was actually questioned by an elder in his church just for putting his arm around a ten-year-old boy while sitting next to him on the couch.)

7. Infection: Many people unreasonably fear contracting the AIDS virus from individuals who have a homosexual past.

   What if he has AIDS? Don't all homosexuals have AIDS? What if he infects me and my family? I had better keep my distance. (Note: not a single AIDS infection has ever been linked to casual contact such as hugging or shaking hands.)

8. Inexperience: Some feel that "ignorance is bliss" when it comes to loving homosexual strugglers.

   I don't know anything about homosexuality; I'll say something stupid or offensive. I don't know how to help this person, so I'm just going to avoid him.

9. Ineligibility: Some people take the position that homosexual promiscuity is a "special sin" for which there is no redemption.

   This person was involved in homosexual behavior, and that sin is unforgivable. He does not deserve God's love or mine.

10. Ignorance: I have heard stories about pastors who refuse to start support groups for homosexuals in their church,

stating, "We don't have that problem here." These pastors refuse to acknowledge the possibility that there could be homosexual strugglers in their congregation.

No one here struggles with homosexuality; I would certainly know about it if they did. Our church is so small, it's unlikely that we have any of those people in our congregation.

Carluzzi recalls an experience he had while speaking in a church a few years ago:

> I introduced four of my brothers in Christ, who shared their stories of how Jesus impacted their lives and began the process of changing their sexual orientation.
>
> At the end of our evening I invited questions from the audience. One woman raised her hand and asked me, "What do these 'homos' call themselves after they become Christians?" A little taken aback by her question, I asked her what she called herself when she became a Christian. Did she introduce herself to new friends as an adulterous or slandering Christian?
>
> I understood what she was asking, but in her mind they were still homosexuals. In some churches, it seems like almost everyone is entitled to a new identity in Christ, regardless of their past, except for the "homos."

Failing to acknowledge the new identity of those who have overcome their homosexuality is one form of homophobia. Furthermore, many churches have applied a double standard to homosexuality. Ed Dobson, pastor of Calvary Church in

Grand Rapids, Michigan, writes, "If a new convert leaves a life of drug addiction, but six months later falls back into the habit, we usually demonstrate patience and understanding. But when it comes to homosexual behavior, if someone reverts to that lifestyle after conversion, we often show little grace."

Another form of homophobia that has penetrated the walls of the church is hypocrisy. As Christians, we often condemn those involved in homosexuality while neglecting to admit that we too have fallen short of God's best for our lives. Gordon Dalbey writes, "When we see homosexuals glossing over their brokenness as if it were just fine, we are simply observing in another man the same charade, the same rationalizing away of sin–albeit different sin–that we ourselves indulge. . . . The conservative witness, however, seems more anxious to proclaim itself 'the Moral Majority' than other fellow sinners. Thus, it bears no saving power for homosexuals, but often provokes their scornful rejection instead."

Furthermore, Christians who believe that the Bible singles out homosexuality as a "special sin" that God hates more than other sins need to reread some of the Bible verses that condemn homosexuality. Steve Bush says:

> Many people believe the Bible singles out homosexuality as a particularly terrible sin because it says in Leviticus that homosexuals should be put to death. But few people have read the rest of this chapter . . . just four verses before this one it says, "If anyone curses his father or mother he must be put to death. He has cursed his father and his mother, his blood will be on his own head."

> I can remember an argument that exploded in my home a while back, and my father tried to shove me through a door and I knocked the door open and hit my dad as hard as I could, knocking him down. I then stormed out of the house and slammed the door.
>
> According to God's law, as some people read it, I should be put to death for this! The point of this chapter in Leviticus is not that we should kill homosexuals; the point is that we are *all* sinners desperately in need of God's grace. Homosexuality is just one of those sins.

While most Christians do not believe that the Bible instructs Christians to kill LGBT people, there are fringe movements, such as Fred Phelps's "God Hates Fags" campaign and Phinehas Priests in a religion known as Christian Identity, that advocate for the death of LGBT people, and they do so in Jesus' name. Keeping in mind that some LGBT people may not be able to make a distinction between these extremists and the attitudes of the Christian majority should help us respond to their anger with a higher degree of patience and understanding. We must also keep in mind that there is some truth to the claims of gay political groups that insist that faith in Christ and hatred for LGBT people go hand in hand.

For example, some scholars believe that opposition to homosexuality was almost nonexistent in most Western societies until Christianity was introduced during the late Roman Empire. They blame the homophobic attitudes that often accompany opposition to homosexuality today on the spread of Christianity during this time.

Whatever the case, there is no question that biblical texts have been used to justify the unjust persecution of LGBT people.

Jesus Loves Me, This I Know

I witnessed the Bible being used as a weapon against LGBT people when the Des Moines City Council announced its decision to consider adding the words "sexual orientation" to our city code a few years ago. I listened in horror as my Christian brothers and sisters stood at the microphone in city hall with Bibles in their hands and informed the "sodomites" in the room that they had better take a liking to fire, because they'll be spending their future in it.

Philip Yancey, in his book *What's So Amazing about Grace?* talks about his experience at a gay-pride march in Washington, D.C. He witnessed a group of Bible-believing Christians shouting derogatory comments at a crowd of homosexuals from the Metropolitan Community Church (which, except for its position on homosexuality, embraces an evangelical theology). Yancey was amazed when the group of homosexuals responded by facing their tormentors and singing the old Sunday-school song "Jesus Loves Me." Yancey writes, "The abrupt ironies in that scene of confrontation struck me. On the one side were Christians defending pure doctrine. . . . On the other side were 'sinners,' many of whom openly admit to homosexual practice. Yet the more orthodox group spewed out hate and the other group sang of Jesus' love."

Even a basic study of Jesus' life reveals the irony of the way that many Christians have treated homosexuals. The Jesus who suffered persecution because he dared to love the very people that his culture oppressed is the same Jesus who started the revolution that today many lesbian and gay people have experienced as oppressive. Yancey writes, "Indeed, for women and other oppressed people, Jesus turned upside down the accepted wisdom of the day. . . . By going out of his way to meet with Gentiles, eat with sinners, and touch the sick, he extended the realm of God's mercy."

Yancey goes on to say that "Jesus went out of his way to embrace the unloved and unworthy, the folks who matter not at all to the rest of society . . . to prove that even 'nobodies' matter infinitely to God." Yancey points out that because of the types of people Jesus gravitated to, he actually defied just about every rule of social propriety in his day. Jesus shared meals with tax collectors, most of whom were viewed as thieves, and routinely stood up for the dignity of those whom no one else would stand up for, like the adulterous woman in John 8, the prostitute in John 12, and those who were afflicted with diseases, such as the blind, the lame, and the lepers.

As I mentioned in chapter 2, people with leprosy were often treated subhumanly, required by law to live outside of town and to keep a six-foot distance from everyone else. Yancey writes, "In Palestine, stern laws enforced the stigma against leprosy: the afflicted had to live outside city walls and yell 'Unclean!' when they approached anyone. Yet Jesus ignored those rules and reclined at the table of a man who wore that stigma as part of his name." A little later on in the book, Yancey writes about the leper who approached Jesus while he was on his way to the synagogue to preach: "I can easily imagine indignation rippling through the crowd when one such outcast walked through them, no doubt given a wide berth, and threw himself at the feet of Jesus. 'Lord, if you are willing, you can make me clean,' he said. Matthew, Mark, and Luke give varying accounts of the scene, but all three include the same explosive sentence: 'Jesus reached out his hand and touched the man.' The crowd must have gasped."

My purpose here is not to say that lesbian and gay people are "nobodies" or to compare them to tax collectors, prostitutes, or lepers. My only intent is to paint a picture of a man who, while on earth, was anything but homophobic. Jesus embraced those whom most people were afraid to get near.

Every single lesbian, gay, bisexual, or transgender person who has become alienated from Jesus' love as a result of the fear and hatred that has been exhibited by those who claim to represent him needs to be shown that the real Jesus had nothing to do with such hatred. In fact, much of his time on earth was spent chastising those who exhibited such judgmental attitudes, referring to them as "vipers" and "hypocrites" (see Matt. 23).

The apostle Paul also makes it clear that God's people are not to pass judgment on those who are outside the church (1 Cor. 5:12–13), yet so many churches persist in their public proclamation of homosexuality as a "special sin." And some continue to insist that Levitical references to homosexuality as a sin deserving of death should be taken literally. Were Jesus to visit our planet again, he would no doubt have some words with these "vipers."

In conclusion, as God's people, we have the capacity to unconditionally love people who are or have been homosexual. But to do so, we must abandon the hypocrisy and the unreasonable fear that holds us back from fully and truly embracing these people in a way that rivals the secular world (1 John 4:18).

We owe the homosexual community some recognition that while some of their hardships may have been caused by promiscuity or poor lifestyle choices on their part, some have been caused by uncaring or uneducated Christians.

We must promise to do better.

4

A God Like Ours

How to address the teaching of homosexuality in the public schools

"Jesus would refuse them."

These four words blasting across the editorial page of the paper instantly caught my attention. I then read in horror as the writer of this letter to the editor of Des Moines' mainstream newspaper unpacked the logic behind his claim that, were Jesus a landlord, he would have refused to rent to a homosexual.

After reading this article, I couldn't help but think of a statement made by ex-gay John Paulk about an experience he'd had at a gay-pride celebration before his conversion. In his book *Not Afraid to Change*, he writes, "People dressed in

Sunday-best clothes held signs saying, TURN OR BURN, FLIP OR FRY, QUEERS GO HOME and ALL GAYS GO TO HELL." John then describes how this affected his view of God and his willingness to consider serving him. He writes, "Why would anyone want to follow a God like theirs?"

While most Christians don't go to quite these extremes when communicating their feelings about homosexuality, the example serves as a reminder that we must use discernment when expressing our beliefs. This is true not only because we are representing the God whose Word makes it clear that it's our *kindness* which leads people to repentance (Rom. 2:4) but also because the gay political movement is fueled by the rhetoric of Christians who are uneducated or insensitive.

Gay media sources that control, to a degree, the worldview of their homosexual demographic are relentless in portraying the religious right as a bunch of homophobic bigots. Christians who have a voice on this subject must keep in mind that gay media types are just waiting for us to say something that could be construed as hateful. As I mentioned in chapter 2, we must heed these rhetorical traps by avoiding common misconceptions about homosexuality (i.e., homosexual attractions are a "choice") and divisive terminology (i.e., referring to homosexuals as "sodomites").

The Safe Schools Campaign

A great example of a movement that's fueled by Christian rhetoric is the effort to indoctrinate public-school children with biased information about homosexuality. The mantra of the Gay, Lesbian, and Straight Education Network (GLSEN), the organization at the helm of this effort, is called Safe Schools. Its foundation is the idea that LGBT students are being ostracized by their peers and that GLSEN's curriculum addresses their struggles.

The curriculum really does address the legitimate needs of LGBT students; for example, freedom from harassment. But it also teaches that homosexuality is an unchangeable condition that must be embraced, instead of presenting information from both sides of the debate and letting students make up their own minds. Absent from GLSEN's teachings is any mention of the thousands of homosexuals who have successfully redirected their sexual orientations through means like counseling and prayer. If they are mentioned, their lives are usually discredited. In some instances, the idea that homosexuals can change is even ridiculed.

GLSEN's strategy is effective because there will always be people, mostly Christians, who don't use discretion when stating their beliefs about homosexual behavior. It is our militancy when dealing with this issue that allows GLSEN to characterize Christians as the perpetuators of hatred toward LGBT students and their curriculum as necessary to combat this hatred.

Take, for example, comments made by Kevin Jennings, GLSEN's founder, during a speech given to the Human Rights Campaign in 1995: "We knew that, confronted with real-life stories of youth who had suffered from homophobia, our opponents would automatically be put on the defensive:

they would have to attack people who had already been victimized once, which put them in a bully position from which it would be hard to emerge looking good."

If we continue to fight the onslaught of homosexual curriculum with hostility toward and ignorance of the legitimate hardships faced by LGBT students, we will not only set ourselves up for political defeat but also alienate the very people we wish to bring into the kingdom of God. Furthermore, the rest of the world, which knows nothing about the dark side of the homosexual political movement or the deceit of those who wish to indoctrinate our school children, will hear the accusations of our opponents and simply assume that *we* are the bad guys.

I was aghast when I read an article from a prominent Christian organization responding to GLSEN's Day of Silence campaign. During this campaign, public school students are encouraged to stay silent for a day as a way of symbolizing the fear experienced by LGBT students who are afraid to speak up for fear of rejection or ridicule. The Christian organization responded by saying that they'd "love for the homosexual side to take this project 24/7/365" and called for extending the day of silence indefinitely to give students a break from "relentless gay propaganda" in their schools.

Beyond the fact that such a statement is politically unwise, how would we expect this statement to be interpreted by LGBT students who really are being ostracized by their peers? Can you imagine what could have been accomplished if, instead of ridiculing those who participated in the event, this organization had acknowledged the legitimacy of the struggle faced by LGBT students and offered a real-life solution to their dilemma?

Instead, what I see coming from many in the Christian community is vehement opposition to the political agenda of groups like GLSEN, occasionally followed by a casual admission that gay kids shouldn't get beat up. *But nobody on our side is actually doing anything about it.*

Many conservatives insist that universal enforcement of antibullying laws already in place will put an end to the problems LGBT kids face, and they oppose singling out gay youth for "special protection." But schools already have many programs in place to address specific problems that students face such as drug abuse (DARE) and learning disabilities ("Special Ed"). Many schools even have nutrition programs that educate kids about obesity. I don't see anything inconsistent about schools offering programs to address the specific issues faced by gay students.

While GLSEN has created an in-school support group called the Gay/Straight Alliance (GSA), which provides a safe environment for young people who otherwise have nowhere to go for support when dealing with their sexuality, conservatives who are watching from the other side are too busy accusing GLSEN of promoting homosexuality to see that many of GLSEN's initiatives, though sometimes dangerous and misleading, are meeting a real need.

In short, gay activists have the lie packaged in tangible solutions for the struggles faced by LGBT students, and Christians have the truth packaged in a laissez-faire admission of their sufferings.

Is it any wonder the lie is winning?

For GLSEN, affirmation of the LGBT students' condition is the cargo, and condemnation of their mistreatment is the vessel on which it sails ahead. Few school districts would open their doors to a group whose stated purpose is to "affirm homosexual behavior." However, doors have a way of just gliding open when you say you want to teach respect. Once you're in the door, you can say whatever you want.

Consider a California group called Initial Images. They receive invitations from secular schools to discuss sonography (ultrasound technology) in science and math classes. Once in the door, they show pictures of babies developing in the womb, pointing out the limbs and beating hearts. By the end of class, most of the students in the room are convinced that abortion is wrong. The group's founder, Chris Bushey, understands the power of his strategy. "I can't walk into a public school with a Bible," he says, "but I can walk in with an ultrasound system."

If we wish to be successful in our attempts to bring God's message of hope for the homosexual into our public schools, we must not go running to the door screaming about the spiritual and physical consequences of homosexual behavior. Rather, we must approach it with a plan to reduce the suffering of LGBT youth in tangible ways. This must be *our* ultrasound system.

Real-Life Solutions

While I am against many of the things that GLSEN teaches, I submit that human psychology, personal experience, and the Bible tell us that emotional congruency is a central element of mental and spiritual health (1 John 1:7). No one, gay, straight, or ex-gay, should feel shunned into silence about what is certainly a traumatic struggle.

Though I disagree with many of the conclusions that Mel White draws in his book *Stranger at the Gate*, I admit he makes some important points, particularly this one: "In spite of their many gifts to me, conservative Christians remained silent about the secret longings of my heart. And though I was surrounded by their loving presence, that same silence left me feeling increasingly isolated and lonely. *In the days of my gay childhood, there was no one who even tried to help clear up my growing confusion, guilt, and fear*" (emphasis added).

Richard Mouw, President of Fuller Theological Seminary in Pasadena, California, said, "My theology of homosexuality, abortion, and sexual immorality is the same as many in the Christian Right. But I am wary of the arrogant and unrepentant spirit that I see in some of these organizations. Christians should remember that one of the reasons the culture is in such bad shape sexually is that we failed in the past to address the issues in a positive, biblical way and instead fostered a sexually oppressive subculture."

It's time that Christians acknowledged the struggles faced by LGBT students and started offering real-life solutions. Everything from name-calling to vandalism is aimed at any young man whose demeanor is even slightly feminine or at any young woman who comes across as "butch" or masculine. Some of these students face misunderstanding, isolation, and sometimes even abandonment by friends and family. Many of these precious lives are lived in desperation or ended in suicide.

So what can be done?

Teachers

- Words like "fag" and "dyke" are hurtful to those who identify themselves as homosexual. Those who use such words often say they are not talking about homosexuals, but use of these words can be hurtful nevertheless. It is not uncommon for some people to reply to a piece of bad news with the phrase, "That's so gay." If you hear these phrases in your classroom, politely remind students that their remarks could be hurtful.
- Put a pink triangle on your door to send the message that your classroom is a safe place for homosexuals. Those who are aware of your position on homosexuality may question your sincerity, but this is a good way to show people around you that opposition to homosexuality is not tantamount to hatred for gays.
- Don't be afraid to talk about homosexuality with your students. You may think that school is not the place to talk about these things; however, as long as organizations like GLSEN are around, people *will* be talking about homosexuality in school. And as long as people are talking about it, you may as well add your voice to

the conversation. In fact, yours may be the only voice offering students an alternative to homosexuality.

Students

- Befriend students who have identified themselves as lesbian or gay. A good way to get a conversation started is to ask questions: "When did you first think you might be gay?" "What has been your greatest challenge since coming out of the closet?" "How has your family reacted to all of this?" Don't ask these questions to try to prove a point, and don't play counselor either. Just listen. You may be surprised by how much you have in common with him or her.
- If you are a college student who lives in a dormitory, you can put a pink triangle on your door to send the message that your dorm floor is a safe place for homosexuals. This may open the door for you to build friendships with lesbian and gay students at your school who may need a friend. Some of your Christian friends may question the triangle: "Why are you supporting homosexuality?" This will give you the opportunity to explain to them that one can take a stand against the mistreatment of homosexuals without supporting homosexuality.
- Respond to news items or editorials in your campus newspaper on the subject of homosexuality. If the item is endorsing homosexuality, write a letter to the editor presenting the opposing viewpoint. But if the item is bashing homosexuals, write a letter in their defense.

(This is the last thing that members of your school's GSA will expect from a Christian student.)

Parents

- Start by teaching your kids that it's ok to befriend someone who is lesbian or gay. A 2003 survey of Christian college students found that only 37 percent had a friend who was lesbian or gay. No wonder gay kids have such a hard time in school! All Christian parents need to teach their children that it's ok to be friends with someone who is lesbian or gay, even if they believe homosexuality is wrong. Notwithstanding that, the emotional and spiritual maturity of the student who would befriend a homosexual must be taken into consideration. Before even considering this suggestion, he or she should be rooted in the Word of God and secure in his or her beliefs about homosexuality.
- Make an effort to get to know the students and teachers who run the school's GSA. As I mentioned in chapter 2, the only image many people have of gays is the militant activist shouting, "We're coming after your children!" But if you take the time to get to know the leaders of your school's GSA, you may be surprised to find out that some of them care about these kids just as much as you do; they simply have a different viewpoint about what's in their best interest.
- When the GSAs do things you don't like, stay calm! The last time a public school in Des Moines hosted an event for its GSA, I received calls from parents who

were just livid. They were so angry that I couldn't even get them to listen long enough for me to explain what needed to be done. All they wanted to talk about was how to sue the school. In some cases, lawsuits may be necessary, but often it can be more effective to create a dialogue with your opponents. Set up a meeting between concerned parents, leaders of the GSA, and the school's counselor. This will give you the opportunity to explain your position and to befriend members of the GSA at the same time. This may also help members of the GSA realize that Christian parents do not always have to be the enemy.

- If your child's school has an annual "diversity day" or any event at which the school's GSA will be allowed to address the student body, ask your child's principal to allow an ex-gay speaker at the event as well. (Information is available on Inqueery's website regarding legislation your school board can pass to require that equal time be given to opposing viewpoints on homosexuality.)

Maybe We're Not All "Freaks"

It's important that real live ex-gay speakers be brought into the schools to tell their stories. Many of the LGBT people who attended my seminar in western Iowa had a poor image of ex-gay people, likely because the only knowledge they had about us is what they had read in pro-gay publications, which usually paint ex-gays as "freaks." But when they met me and found that I was just like them in many ways, many shifted their view of ex-gays.

Maybe we're not all freaks.

When homosexually oriented students are confronted with information on sexual reorientation, they need to be shown a healthy image of ex-gays or they may never consider pursuing their heterosexual potential. Furthermore, it's important to develop ex-gay resources that can be used in private- or public-school classrooms and on college campuses (such as those available at www.Inqueery.com). We must address the legitimate struggles of students who self-identify as LGBT, while maintaining objectivity about the circumstances that can lead to the development of a homosexual orientation and the potential for change.

Many people have questioned the rationale of addressing sexuality issues in school, claiming that schools should be teaching reading, writing, and arithmetic, nothing more. The most common objection to my organization is that homosexuality is a "moral issue, and moral issues should not be taught at school." However, despite the best efforts of the many Christian organizations that are working to preserve the integrity of the family unit, the traditional family, as we know it, is continuing to decay. If God's people will not support the inclusion of materials in the public schools that address issues of moral significance, where will sexually confused teenagers whose parents choose not to discuss moral issues get their information? They will continue to have only biased materials and support groups to refer to for help with their struggle.

The state of affairs in our public schools is truly an example of Christians losing the battle for the hearts and minds of LGBT people because *we have failed to love them first.* But it's not too late. It is time for the church not only to recognize the need to address these issues in public schools but also to take an active role in selecting the materials and shaping the discussion.

Only then will we begin to see the biased discussion of homosexual issues in our public schools put to an end. And only then will those in the LGBT community consider getting to know a God like ours.

5

What Does Science Say?

A look at the science behind homosexuality

After the speaker's concluding remarks, the audience of college students erupted with applause. I pushed my way through the crowd, desperate to determine what effect the speaker, who insisted that homosexuality is genetic, had had on the college group.

When I got to the edge of the crowd, I forced my way into a clique of students who were discussing this topic. "So you think it's for sure genetic?" I asked. "Oh, it's got to be," was the reply. "Anyone who has actually studied the science behind human sexuality wouldn't even ask that question."

I submit that it might be a good idea to do just that, and if, on the off chance, we ever bump into this particular student, we'll be prepared to enter into an intelligent discussion about what science has said about homosexuality.

In this chapter, I'll outline the claims that have been made by the three most well-known scientific studies on homosexuality. The first study was conducted by Simon LeVay, whose research claimed to have found a "difference in hypothalamic structure between heterosexual and homosexual men."

The second study was conducted by John M. Bailey and Richard Pillard, who studied the prevalence of homosexuality among biological twins and adopted brothers.

The third study was conducted by Dean Hamer, who claimed to have found a "linkage between DNA markers on the X chromosome and male sexual orientation."

All of these researchers, except for Bailey, are self-identified gay men.

Simon LeVay

In 1991, Simon LeVay studied the brains of the cadavers of thirty-five men, nineteen of whom he believed were homosexuals and sixteen of whom he believed were heterosexuals. (LeVay told *Science* magazine that he had "assumed" the sexual orientation of some of his subjects.)

LeVay found a group of neurons in the hypothalamus that appeared to be twice as large in the heterosexual men as in the homosexual men. (The hypothalamus has been associated with the regulation of hormone release and reproductive behavior. It has been called the "most vital structure for motivation and emotion" in the human body.) He then suggested that the size of this group of neurons, called the INAH3, might have something to do with sexual orientation.

Note that LeVay never claimed to have found a genetic cause for homosexuality. LeVay said, upon completing his work, "It's important to stress what I didn't find. I did not prove that homosexuality is genetic, or find a genetic cause for being gay. I didn't show that gay men are born that way, the most common mistake people make in interpreting my work."

Some of LeVay's peers also questioned his research, noting that changes in brain structure could have been the *result* of homosexual behavior, rather than the cause. Dr. Kenneth Klivington of the Saulk Institute stated that there is a body of evidence that shows the brain's neural networks reconfigure themselves in response to certain experiences. Therefore, the difference in homosexual brain structure may be a result of behavioral and environmental conditions.

In a study published in March of 2001, William Byne and a group of his collegues attempted to replicate LeVay's study but were not able to do so. The researchers said, "Although there was a trend for INAH3 to occupy a smaller volume in homosexual men than in heterosexual men, there was no difference in the number of neurons within the nucleus based on sexual orientation."

Bailey and Pillard

J. Michael Bailey and Richard Pillard published a study in the *Archives of General Psychiatry* in December of 1991 on the prevalence of homosexuality among twins. They studied

56 pairs of identical twins, where at least one brother was homosexual, and found that 29 of them (52 percent) were both homosexual. They also found that 12 of 54 pairs of fraternal twins (22 percent) were both homosexual and 6 out of 57 pairs of adopted brothers (11 percent) were both homosexual. Bailey and Pillard, therefore, concluded that homosexuality has a genetic cause.

Biologist Anne Fausto-Stirling of Brown University, wasn't so sure. She said, "In order for such a study to be at all meaningful, you'd have to look at twins raised apart." As I mentioned in chapter 1, environmental factors such as a child's relationship to his peers and sexual abuse or molestation can affect sexual development. Therefore, it would be impossible for Dr. Bailey and Dr. Pillard to determine whether it was genetics or environmental factors that caused the twins' homosexuality unless the twins were separated. Furthermore, if it were genes and not environment that caused the twins' homosexuality, one would expect 100 percent of the identical twins to both be homosexual instead of just 52 percent. Dr. Bailey seemed to agree. He wrote, "There must be something in the environment to yield the discordant twins."

The most powerful refutation of this study, however, is the researcher's inability to replicate his own work. In a study released in March of 2000, Dr. Bailey and a group of his colleagues used an Australian population of twins to conduct a similar twin study with even lower concordance numbers. The researchers studied the largest carefully ascertained twin sample ever assembled for such a study. They found that, for women, only 24 percent were both homosexual and, of the men they studied, only 20 percent were both homosexual.

Upon completing this study the researchers said, "Consistent with several studies of siblings, we found that sexual orientation is familial. In contrast to most prior twin studies of sexual orientation, however, ours did not provide statistically significant support for the importance of genetic factors for that trait. This does not mean that our results support heritability estimates of zero, though our results do not exclude them either."

Dr. Warren Throckmorton, an associate professor of psychology at Grove City College who has done research on homosexuality, was taken aback by Bailey's own admission that genetics may have no impact on sexual orientation at all. He said, "Heritability near zero? This is a pretty amazing statement! And one that no one has heard in the popular media."

Dean Hamer

Dr. Dean Hamer of the National Cancer Institute studied forty pairs of homosexual brothers and found that thirty-three of the brothers had the same pattern at the tip of the X chromosome known as the Xq28. Hamer estimated that this pattern was responsible for homosexual development in 64 percent of the brothers he studied.

As in the LeVay study, it is hard to determine whether these changes were the result or the cause of homosexual behavior.

George Ebers of the University of Western Ontario attempted to replicate Hamer's study. He examined fifty-two pairs of gay brothers and found no connection between the pattern of the Xq28 and the homosexuality of his subjects.

Dr. Hamer himself wrote, "These genes do not cause people to become homosexuals . . . the biology of personality is much more complicated than that."

What I find the most interesting about this particular study is that even after Hamer's comments to the contrary, a few media outlets ran stories with headlines suggesting that a gay gene had been unmistakably discovered. The *Wall Street Journal*'s headline read "Research Points toward a Gay Gene," and the Associated Press wrote "Study Finds Genetic Link to Homosexuality."

The American Psychiatric Association (APA)

The Diagnostic and Statistical Manual, also known as the DSM, is the official list of mental disorders that all mental health professionals refer to when diagnosing patients.

The first version, released in 1952, listed homosexuality as a sociopathic personality disturbance. In 1968, the second version (DSM II) reclassified homosexuality as a sexual deviancy. Soon afterward, gay protestors began picketing at the APA's annual conventions, demanding that homosexuality be removed from the list completely. In 1973, after intensive debate and numerous disturbances by gay activists, the APA decided to remove homosexuality from its next manual (DSM III).

What followed was a swarm of outrage from psychiatrists within the APA who disagreed with the decision and demanded that the issue be reconsidered. In 1974, a referendum was called and approximately 40 percent of the APA's membership voted to put homosexuality back into the DSM. Since a majority was not achieved to reverse the decision, homosexuality remains omitted from the APA's Diagnostic and Statistical Manual.

To the LGBT community, this omission from the DSM was a logical move. They felt that, absent from any nonbiased social-science research to prove that homosexuality is inherently pathological, the only thing that had been keeping homosexuality in the DSM was societal prejudice. However, many in the scientific community have criticized the APA's decision to remove homosexuality from the DSM, claiming its motives were more political than scientific.

Dr. Ronald Bayer, author of the book *Homosexuality and American Psychiatry*, writes:

> The entire process, from the first confrontation organized by gay demonstrators to the referendum demanded by orthodox psychiatrists, seemed to violate the most basic expectations about how questions of science should be resolved.
>
> Instead of being engaged in sober discussion of data, psychiatrists were swept up in a political controversy. The result was not a conclusion based on an approximation of the scientific truth as dictated by reason, but was instead an action demanded by the ideological temper of the times.

Along these same lines, a recent radio documentary on the subject of homosexuality revealed that the president-elect of the APA in 1973, Dr. John P. Speigel, was a "closeted homosexual with a very particular agenda."

Another of the reasons APA members were so quick to vote in favor of homosexuality's removal from the DSM, according to Dr. Joseph Nicolosi, is that many in the psychiatric profession had "failed to identify, with certainty, the psychodynamic causes of homosexuality, and consequently to devise a reasonably successful treatment for it." (It should be noted that although the psychiatric profession as a whole has failed in treating homosexuals, there are still many psychotherapists who report great success in such treatment.)

While the medical profession in general has done much to advance our knowledge of human functioning, in some cases it seems that modern medicine seeks to recognize or diagnose only those problems that it can remedy. I found this out a few years ago when I experienced an unexplained twitching in my eye. (The medical term is "blesphorospasm.") I visited a general practitioner, two optometrists, an ophthalmologist, and a neurologist and underwent a thirteen-hundred-dollar MRI scan only to be told I had no problem. Although a few of the physicians were able to name my symptom, none could tell me, with certainty, what was causing it. It wasn't until I visited a doctor friend of my dad's (whose alternative methods were not even recognized as legitimate by my insurance company) that my problem was diagnosed and corrected. And, I might add, he charged me only forty-five dollars.

Gordon Dalbey writes, "I am convinced that the American Psychiatric Society [*sic*] *removed* homosexuality from its list of mental illnesses simply because the psychiatrists were tired of failing in their human efforts to heal it." He suggests that the reason much of secular psychiatry has failed in treating those with unwanted homosexual desires is that it has ignored the spiritual component of this process. Dalbey points out that homosexuality is something that "only the Father God can heal."

Another factor in the APA's decision to remove homosexuality from its list may have been the *perception* that there were not many homosexuals who desired therapy to change their orientation. This perception may have been fueled by the fact that ex-gays were not nearly as vocal in 1973 as we are now.

While I agree that homosexuality is not a mental illness per se, I take issue with the fact that the APA and many other professional organizations have moved far beyond just saying that homosexuality is not an illness, and instead are now saying that reorientation therapy could potentially "harm" someone trying to change from gay to straight. Groups like the American Psychological Association, the National Association of Social Workers, and the American Academy of Pediatrics have upset a large portion of their membership by rejecting the idea that homosexuals can change.

In doing this, most of the major psychological associations have turned their backs on people like me. But there are still hundreds of mental-health experts successfully treating homosexuals; they just aren't advertising it. This is because doing so could get them in trouble, if some gay activists have their way. There has been a move in the APA to make treatment of homosexuality a violation of professional conduct for a psychiatrist, even if it's done at the patient's request.

Nature or Nurture?

Some people have exaggerated or misrepresented the findings of the studies referenced in this chapter in an attempt to prove that homosexuality is influenced only by genetics. As Jeffrey Satinover writes, "There is no evidence that shows that homosexuality is genetic–and none of the research itself claims there is. Only the press and certain researchers do, when speaking in sound bites to the public."

While some believe that homosexuality is determined purely by genetics, others believe that homosexuality is determined purely by environment. However, many researchers have come to the conclusion that sexual orientation is likely determined by a complex interaction between a person's genetic makeup and their environment. (This will be explained further in the next chapter.) Even the American Psychological Association asserts that "There are numerous theories about the origins of a person's sexual orientation; most scientists today agree that sexual orientation is most likely the result of a complex interaction of environmental, cognitive and biological factors. In most people, sexual orientation is shaped at an early age." And the American Psychiatric Association wrote: "Currently there is a renewed interest in searching for biological etiologies for homosexuality. However, to date there are no replicated scientific studies supporting any specific biological etiology for homosexuality."

Whatever the case, we know from the testimonies of thousands that homosexuality is a changeable condition. Stanton Jones, a psychologist who is now provost at Wheaton College, states, "Every secular study of change has shown some success rate, and persons who testify to substantial healings by God are legion."

6

What Causes Homosexuality?

Listen to me, you that pursue righteousness, you that seek the LORD. Look to the rock from which you were hewn, and to the quarry from which you were dug.

–Isaiah 51:1

Although the human brain is far too complex for a single theory to explain the development of homosexual attractions, the combination of psychology and human experience have made some interesting discoveries.

More than a hundred years of psychological research and the attempts of science to provide a biological explanation for homosexuality have continued to support a developmental theory; that is, homosexual orientation is developed during the formative years of life as a response to both internal (genetics) and external (environmental) circumstances.

The seemingly automatic process by which nonsexual attraction to members of one's gender morphs into a sexual desire for one's opposite gender during puberty is not automatic at all. It is the culmination of an entire childhood of affirmation, attention, affection, approval, discipline, instruction, touch, time, and nurturing from a member of one's own gender, usually the same-sex parent.

Research has found that when a child's needs for same-sex affirmation and identification are met, the child's need to identify with his or her same-sex counterparts will lessen. By the time the child reaches puberty, his or her same-gender peers seem familiar and boring, and attractions to the opposite sex kick in. Dr. Joseph Nicolosi writes, "We do not sexualize what we identify with; when we identify with someone, we are no longer sexually attracted to them. It is always to the other-than-ourselves that we are drawn."

According to Dr. Nicolosi, a child's relationship with his or her same-sex parent is generally the child's primary means of identification with and affirmation from his or her gender. "As very young infants, both boys and girls are first identified with the mother, who is the first and primary source of nurturance and care. However, whereas the girl *maintains* primary identification with the mother, the boy later has the additional developmental task of shifting identification from the mother to the [father]."

Dr. Nicolosi goes on to say that if the father is warm and receptive, the boy will be encouraged to disidentify from the feminine and identify with the masculine. The boy will then become masculine-identified and most probably heterosexual. "In freeing himself from his bond with mother, the boy needs help in becoming fully male. He needs to know who he is, and only another man can tell him."

In the same way, a warm and receptive mother will encourage her daughter to become feminine-identified and most likely heterosexual. When the relationship between a boy and his father, or a girl and her mother, suffers, the child may not identify with his or her same-sex parent. This can create an unconscious drive for gender identification that follows him or her into adolescence. This unconscious drive for gender identification becomes eroticized (turns sexual) as a child develops his or her sexual identity. By the time a child reaches adolescence, the child may experience sexual attractions to members of his or her own sex. In short, an emotional need becomes an erotic desire.

Andy Comiskey, who works with people overcoming homosexuality, writes, "In joining with the same sex erotically, the needy child within seeks in adult form the affirmation and emotional intimacy from the same sex that was never properly attained in childhood." Comiskey says that in the majority of his clients, "gay sex wasn't really the motivating factor in their homosexual pursuits, while same-sex intimacy was, [and therefore reflected] an emotional need as opposed to an erotic one."

In his book *Coming Out Straight*, psychotherapist and author Richard Cohen writes, "A man is looking for his father's love through another man, and a woman is looking for her mother's love through another woman." This is why many people (that's many, not all) who experience homosexual attractions report poor relationships with their same-sex parent or primary caregiver while growing up. There is little controversy surrounding the belief that a child's parents play a significant role in his or her emotional development, yet when theorists suggest that the same applies to sexual development, they sometimes receive opposition from those in the lesbian and gay community who believe that sexuality is determined purely by genetics.

It is very important to note that I'm not trying to suggest that all LGBT people have suffered from poor relationships with their parents. However, evidence points to a strong correlation between a child's early same-sex relationships and the formation of his or her sexual orientation. A 1994 questionnaire, which asked 117 gay men questions about their childhood, found that

- 86 percent indicated little or no time spent with their fathers during their childhood.
- 63 percent said their fathers were not considerate of their needs.
- 50 percent believed their fathers did not love them.
- 45 percent reported that their fathers belittled or humiliated them.
- 44 percent felt their fathers neglected them.
- 40 percent said their fathers were disinterested and detached.
- 39 percent said they hated their fathers.

Only eighteen out of the 117 men questioned (15 percent) described their relationship with their father as affectionate or warm. In a study of forty homosexual males, researcher J. H. Brown reported not a single case in which a homosexual male had an affectionate relationship with his father.

Infinite Influences

While a child's relationship with his same-sex parent is believed to play the most prevalent role in determining sexual orientation, an almost infinite number of influences can contribute to homosexual development.

Some children may have had an excellent relationship with their same-gender parent but experienced rejection from their same-gender peers or were victims of sexual molestation. *Anything* that creates a sense of disconnection between a child and his or her gender, consciously or unconsciously, can stifle gender identification and potentially create homosexual attractions. Here are some of the most common influences, the first two of which have already been mentioned in this chapter:

- *Rejection by one's same-gender parents or peers* (real or perceived lack of physical and emotional closeness with one's same-sex parent, caregiver, or peers during the formative years of development)
- *Sexual molestation*
- *Temperament* (a child's natural inclination to be sensitive or artistic versus athletic or mechanical)

- *An abnormally close relationship with one's opposite-sex parent*
- *Lack of identification with one's gender* (having no sense of "belonging" to one's gender)
- *Genetics*

For easy reference, I will italicize each of these factors when they appear in the following paragraphs. It's important to note that no single factor will guarantee homosexual development; rather, it is the interrelationship of multiple factors that can cause homosexuality.

Since *rejection by one's same-gender parents or peers* is often the prelude to the development of homosexual attractions, any inborn characteristic that might perpetuate this rejection can contribute to homosexuality. For example, a boy who is born with a more artistic or sensitive *temperament* might have a more athletic father who has a hard time connecting with him. The father may intentionally or unknowingly reject his son.

Corey tells of how he would play catch with his dad and brother when he was younger. Corey's brother, Lee, was a typical jock–coordinated, athletic–and much like his dad. Corey, on the other hand, was sensitive, artistic, and musical. When his dad pitched the baseball to him, he would often miss the catch, terrified of the fastball zooming toward his face. Corey's dad would respond by saying, "Why can't you be more like your brother?" For Corey, this was the point at which he became disconnected from his father and from masculinity in general.

Nathaniel, who also struggles with same-sex attractions, writes, "My memories of doing things with dad include hunting, fishing, bowling, and carpentry. All things I was essentially bad at. All I ever remember getting from my dad during those activities was criticism or punishing silence. It was humiliating."

Another factor that can affect sexual development is an *abnormally close relationship with one's opposite-sex parent.* For males, attraction to men can be intensified by a repulsion to women. If a boy had a mother or other female caretaker who smothered him because of her neediness, the development of heterosexuality could be interrupted. An abnormally close mother-son relationship can cause a male child to, unconsciously, fear women later in life. The last thing he would want is a relationship with someone who is anything like the woman he despises.

I had a physically present but emotionally distant father. He did his best to love me, but his love was overshadowed by periodic fits of rage when things didn't go his way. In response to his lack of emotional stability, I never allowed myself to bond with him. My inability to connect with my father left me spending most of my childhood relating to my mother, the only emotionally safe person in the household. My consequent overidentification with her created in me a distaste for the feminine that I have had to work at overcoming.

In the case of a female, a distaste for men can be created by an abnormally close father-daughter relationship. Also, physical, emotional, psychological, or sexual abuse may have taken place during her formative years that taught her to hate men. Dr. Carol Ahrens, a therapist who has done extensive work with women, writes that for girls who were sexually abused, "the association of the male body with a childhood trauma may make the thought of sex with men repulsive or frightening."

Oftentimes, a male child whose father is brutal and insensitive will reject his father's masculinity. He will unconsciously say to himself, "If this is what it means to be a man, I don't want anything to do with it." In such a case, *he will be prevented from identifying with his gender.* This is extremely significant because the child who rejects his father's masculinity rejects his own masculinity as well, likely favoring the more sensitive and thoughtful characteristics that he sees in his mother. In the same way, a girl whose mother is brutal and insensitive and whose father is sensitive and thoughtful may be compelled to reject her femininity and identify instead with dad and masculinity.

Sometimes, when a parent who desired a female child gives birth to a male (or vice-versa), the child is rejected for being the "wrong" sex. For example, a mother who desperately wanted a male child might give her daughter a shorter haircut and dress her in boyish clothing. As soon as the child realizes that her femininity has been rejected by her mother, she may reject it as well.

I have said many times in this book that there is no one gene that causes homosexuality (see chapter 5). However, I believe that genetics do play a role in the development of homosexuality to the degree that they can influence environmental factors.

For example, many basketball players possess inherited traits such as height, agility, muscle strength, good reflexes, and speed that predispose them to be athletes. But not everyone possessing these traits becomes a basketball player or even has the desire to become one, although it does make it more likely that they will.

Some boys may be born with characteristics that are considered feminine, or girls may be born with a more masculine appearance or demeanor. But that does not guarantee that they will develop homosexual attractions. It does, however, make it more likely that they will.

People tend to embrace those individuals who best represent the stereotypes associated with their gender. Those who posses opposite-sex characteristics are sometimes at a heightened risk of being rejected by their same-sex parents or peers, which can stifle gender identification. These children are also more likely to get called names like "fag" or "dyke," which sometimes become self-fulfilling prophecies.

Jack Morlan, an ex-gay man, writes, "[Growing up] I felt isolated from my peers. Because I was overweight, other kids called me 'Porky,' . . . I wasn't athletic and didn't fit in with the jocks."

Although there are many homosexuals who like sports, a disproportionate percentage of male homosexuals seem to have a more artistic, sensitive temperament. Dr. Nicolosi refers to the average prehomosexual male as the "'kitchen window boy,' who looks out at his peers playing aggressively and, what appears to him, dangerously."

Of the 117 men who participated in the questionnaire referenced earlier in this chapter, a disproportionate number of them identified with behaviors generally associated with sensitive temperaments:

- 85 percent avoided physical fights.
- 65 percent did not participate in group or competitive games.
- 61 percent were more comfortable with girls growing up.
- 50 percent were excessively fearful of injury.
- 47 percent played mostly with girls before puberty.
- 38 percent played most often with girls' toys or games.

When asked to describe their temperaments, 78 percent of the men considered themselves to be "sensitive," while only 4 percent considered themselves "mechanical." In a study conducted by gay researcher Dean Hamer, 78 percent of heterosexual men said they enjoyed playing sports "very much" as a child, while only 8 percent of the homosexual men said they enjoyed sports "very much." Similarly, a survey of homosexually oriented females found that almost 90 percent identified with masculine activities instead of feminine activities during childhood.

Growing up in a culture that calls sensitive attributes "feminine" or "sissy" makes the essential task of bonding with one's same-gender peers during childhood extremely difficult for boys with these attributes. Furthermore, children who are born with sensitive temperaments, whether male or female, are more likely to internalize even minor forms of rejection from their same-gender peers, which heightens the possibility that they may experience same-gender attractions.

In fact, sensitive children may perceive rejection that's not even there. This is why boys who have a very strong father presence in their lives can still develop homosexual attractions. Their temperament will not allow them to fully receive their father's love. In the same way, a boy can have a father who is distant and uncaring, or no father at all, and still experience heterosexual development because there was another male figure for him to identify with, such as a grandparent, a neighbor, or his peer group. The same is true of females. The concept that is at work here is called surrogacy, which I will define and discuss further in the next chapter.

7

How Does Change Happen?

With man this is impossible, but with God all things are possible.

–Matthew 19:26 (NKJV)

By this point in the book, you should already have at least a general idea of what is required to overcome homosexual attractions. I have touched on it, at least briefly, in earlier chapters.

Before getting started, I feel it's important to note that I do not claim to present an all-inclusive representation of current psychotherapeutic theory on the process of overcoming homosexual attractions. I am merely giving you a *taste* of what's out there, and then expanding on those methods that have been the most helpful to me. (Because the causes and methods for overcoming transgenderism vary from the causes and methods for overcoming homosexuality, transgenderism will not be addressed in this section. Resources for individuals wishing to overcome transgenderism can be found in the resource list at the back of this book.)

In the past, some individuals seeking to change their sexual orientation were often subjected to painful methods of therapy. For example, doctors would show gay men nude pictures of other males while administering emetine (also known as ipecac) to produce nausea. Doctors also tried administering electric shocks to male patients who became aroused by the pictures. The purpose of the therapy was to produce in the patient a profound distaste for, or aversion toward, homosexuality. These treatments were not necessarily harmful, but they were certainly not effective either. Today, treatment is far less tormenting and much more successful.

When you consider that homosexuality is caused by an inability to identify with one's gender during childhood, it only makes sense that the struggler's success at eliminating homosexual attractions will depend on his or her ability to retrieve this identification and affirmation later in life.

Dr. Elizabeth Moberly, author of *Homosexuality: A New Christian Ethic*, writes, "Homosexuality . . . needs to be solved through relationships. The solution of same-sex deficits is to be sought through the medium of . . . nonsexual relationships with members of the same sex."

Jason, who grew up with homosexual attractions, writes:

For years, I tried to hide my growing emotional insecurity and my secret attraction to men. I knew I couldn't tell anyone.

I had a dream that I was involved in homosexual behavior. I woke up scared and confused. After that, I recognized a strong desire to be physically close to my male peers. I felt there was something very wrong with me.

Later on I learned that I did not have to be gay. My homosexual desires began to fade away as I reconnected with my own gender through close but nonsexual friendships with other men.

Psychologist Gerard Van Den Aardweg, in his book, *Homosexuality and Hope*, writes, "Man has a natural drive to identify with his gender. A boy wants to belong to the world of other boys and men, a girl to other girls and women. A longing for being recognized as one of the boys (or girls) is also inherent in boys and girls with inferiority feelings concerning their masculinity or femininity respectively."

As I've mentioned before, anything that creates a sense of disconnection between a child and his or her gender can cause homosexual attractions. Along these same lines, I've found that anything that creates a sense of connection or reconciliation with one's gender can eliminate homosexual attractions. This connection can manifest itself in many ways. The influences that have been the most potent for me are:

- Nonsexual touch from members of my gender
- Surrogacy (substitute parenthood)
- Camaraderie with members of my gender

Nonsexual Touch

If you consider that touch is one of the primary ways that one receives love from parents during the formative years, it makes sense that those who feel rejected by or alienated from their parents didn't receive much touch from them during their infancy.

Dr. Carol Ahrens writes this about one of her patients: "[Gretchen received] no hugging, no intimate talking, no play. So hungry was Gretchen for affection that at night she would deliberately throw her bedclothes off, then pretend to be sleeping, knowing that when Mom came to check on her, she would have to rearrange the covers. As she did so, Gretchen could feel her mother's hands, if only for a moment, touching her and brushing against her. That was her main source of maternal touch."

A friend of mine tells this story: "I came home from work one day and my twelve-year-old son was sitting at the kitchen counter. He asked me, 'Dad can I show you a few new wrestling moves I learned on the trampoline?' I told him I was too tired and needed some time to relax from a hard day of work. He pressed me and said, 'Dad, ah come on, you don't want me to be gay, do ya?'"

Same-sex touch is a prerequisite for healthy heterosexuality because it works as a bonding agent between children and their gender. In fact, it is well-documented that in many primitive cultures, adult male homosexuality does not exist because boys go through a rite of passage with the older men of a village. Though some of the activities that take place are painful and even grotesque (which I am *not* recommending), each of them is accompanied by some form of touch.

Between the ages of nine and fourteen, boys go through what is called the "body longing stage." This is when boys crave physical affection from their fathers and their same-sex peers. During this time, boys will hit, punch, wrestle, horse around, and smack each other on the butt.

In his book *Wild at Heart*, John Eldredge writes about the importance of touch during the formative years:

> So let me tell you of my favorite event of the day. It comes late in the evening, at bedtime, after the boys have brushed their teeth and we've said our family prayers. As I'm tucking them in, one of my boys will ask, "Dad, can we snuggle tonight?" Snuggle time is when I'll cuddle up next to them on a bed that's really not big enough for both of us–and that's the point, to get very close–and there in the dark we'll just sort of talk. Sometimes it breaks into tickling, other times it's a chance for them to ask some serious questions about life. But whatever happens, what matters most is what's going on beneath all that: intimacy, closeness, connection.

For many males, the need for same-sex touch gets fulfilled during participation in team sports, in which it is okay for guys to touch each other in nonsexual ways without being called "homosexual."

Recently, I came across a website on the Internet that humorously asked, "When would you hug another male?"

and provides three choices. The author of the question then suggests, in a tongue-and-cheek manner, that all "real men" would answer C.

A. If he's your father and one of you has a fatal disease.
B. If you're performing the Heimlich maneuver.
C. If you're a professional football player and a teammate scores the goal to win the World Cup, provided that you also pound him fraternally with your fist hard enough to cause fractures.

Nonsexual touch among same-sex individuals can be referred to as "homosocial" behavior. Homosocial behavior is one way that males connect to and identify with each other during the formative years.

When a boy's need for same-sex touch is met, his desire to be close to men physically will slowly fade. However, those of us who weren't "athletic enough" as children, or who were rejected for whatever reason, probably did not receive the healthy same-sex touch we needed. We are stuck in the "body longing" stage and require touch from other males, even as adults, to complete our development. The process is similar for females.

In the book *Unwanted Harvest*, Mona Riley writes, "Children who have not had healthy relating with their same-sex parent or surrogate and who thus approach adolescence with a severe deficit in same-sex bonding may continue to seek the intimacy they were denied."

But there is hope! Lenny Carluzzi writes:

> I avoided contact as a boy, so all the body contact that boys experience during physical activities simply was not a part of my childhood. But while attending a Christian discipleship program as a young adult, I was thrown into a dorm room with three other males my age.
>
> I'll never forget the first time a bunch of us guys threw all our mattresses on the floor to wrestle and throw pillows just for fun. I felt like one of the guys, and it was the first adult body contact that did not end up in orgasm. This kind of roughhousing did a world of good for my self-esteem, and it made up for years of isolation from my same-sex peers.

I had a similar experience while camping with some of my Christian friends in Colorado. We decided it would be fun to try to fit four guys into a three-man tent. It was healing because we were physically close to each other, but it was healing also because they trusted me enough to let me get close to them despite their awareness of my homosexual struggle. My homosexuality was not even an afterthought that night, for them or for me.

Touch can be used as a tool to recover the love that either was not offered by the homosexual struggler's mom or dad or was not properly internalized by the struggler while growing up. In order to facilitate this kind of healing, a struggler's parent, or a trusted friend playing the role of parent, will hold the struggler as they would hold a child. If the parent offers verbal affirmation at the same time, it will further enhance a struggler's healing by building self-esteem. For example, the person holding the struggler can say things like, "You are a bright, handsome man [or beautiful woman]," or, "I'm so proud of you."

It is important that this process is not forced. If the person holding the struggler cannot be sincere, it is best to leave this particular method alone. Also, if the struggler is being held by someone other than his or her own parent, the holder's spouse should be made aware of what is taking place and why. (You might just want to let those involved read this chapter.)

Some research suggests that physical touch can also be used to reeducate the neurology of the brain concerning physical attractions. In chapter 5, I cited some research from the Saulk Institute that shows that the brain's neural networks may actually reconfigure themselves in response to certain experiences. The study found that in people who read Braille after becoming blind, the area of the brain controlling the reading finger grew larger. According to Dr. Kenneth Klivington, "It's a feedback loop: the brain influences behavior, behavior shapes experience, experience affects the organization of the brain, and so forth."

So it is with sexual behavior. Erotic, sexual touch with someone of our own gender reinforces the connection between same-gender intimacy and sex. This stifles our ability to internalize affirmation from males in a way that will quench our same-gender attractions. According to Dr. Nicolosi, "Those men who have been less sexually active have better prognoses. Considering the habit-forming nature of sexual behavior, the more homosexually active the client is, the more difficult the course of treatment."

On the other hand, fraternal, nonsexual touch from members of our gender will forge a connection between male intimacy and *friendship* (camaraderie) that is vital to the process of overcoming homosexual attractions. When a struggler can learn to be physically close to members of his gender without becoming sexually aroused, he may experience the kind of connection that he needs to heal the wounds of his past and transition into heterosexuality. At first, even fraternal love may evoke an erotic response, but as the brain is rewired to receive touch without also receiving sex, that will change.

After receiving his first ever nonsexual hug, one ex-gay man said, "I'd never been hugged by a man in the right way, you know, without it being a sexual thing. . . . I got it all wrong in homosexuality. But at [my support group], I got it right. For the first time a man hugged me and I felt real affirmation–as if someone was proud of me."

Nonsexual intimacy in any form will extinguish homosexual desires, and I have found touch to be one of the most potent ways to facilitate this connection. While nonsexual touch from my heterosexual friends has been of incredible value to me, I have also experienced healing through healthy hugs with other homosexual strugglers. But remember, touch is a bonding agent and can serve to perpetuate unhealthy emotional dependencies when it takes place outside of an understanding of healthy boundaries. Also, it is best that strugglers are fully clothed while hugging. Don't get physically close to another struggler who is not wearing a shirt or is in skimpy pajamas.

It is also important to note that attachment will occur when touch takes place. As a result, one may become ultrasensitive to affirmation or rejection (real or perceived) from his or her counterpart. Strugglers who have sensitive temperaments may perceive rejection that doesn't really exist. The struggler who feels rejected must resist the urge to withdraw, process the emotions, and then move on. Sometimes, setting boundaries in the relationship may help prevent the struggler from feeling rejected when the person who is helping him or her heal is not available. It will also help prevent the healer from being taken advantage of by an overly needy struggler.

It should be noted that extended periods of physical touch have the power to draw out repressed emotions. This is a good thing as long as the struggler is prepared to work through whatever issues may arise. It is also important to note that extended periods of physical touch, sometimes called "holding therapy," should only take place between a homosexual struggler and his or her parents or a trusted friend. Therapists should never hold their clients, nor should homosexual strugglers hold each other. (For more cautions regarding the use of physical touch, see chapters 10 and 12 of Richard Cohen's book *Coming Out Straight*.)

While I recognize the dangers of encouraging homosexual strugglers to be physically close to members of their own gender, I believe that a lack of touch only intensifies a homosexual struggler's longing for affection, which will eventually erupt as sexual temptation. This puts the struggler right back where he or she started.

Human beings consist of body, soul, and spirit. It only makes sense that our healing must take place in all three areas.

In fact, Scripture recounts for us more than one instance in which touch accompanied Jesus' healing of someone.

If you know someone who is in the process of overcoming homosexual attractions, just being willing to initiate a hug for the first time can make a world of difference. Then, based on his or her response, decide whether to continue doing so in the future. It is possible that he or she may not be ready or willing to receive this kind of love just yet, but you won't know until you try.

During the early stages of my change from gay to straight, there was no one in my home state of Iowa whom I felt comfortable going to when I needed a hug. So where did I find hugs? I would use my credit card to charge hundreds of dollars worth of plane tickets to my mentor's home in Seattle. Lenny welcomed me in his arms each time, but I would always joke with him when I got there, "Lenny, this had better be a really good hug; after all, it cost me three hundred dollars!" It is my hope that this book will help prevent other homosexual strugglers from having to resort to such expensive hugs.

For many individuals who have homosexual pasts, the concept of receiving touch outside of a sexual relationship is unheard of. Lenny wrote about his experience after deciding to leave behind his homosexuality: "I wish I could say I was able to end my sexual activity instantly, but the kind of love that I needed to heal was not available to me in the closed Christian environment that I was thrown into. My homosexual relationships still held the only tangible source of touch and love I had known. A love I was yet to see coming from God's people."

Lenny's inability to access the kind of love he needed was further perpetuated by his fear of asking for what he needed. "I didn't know how to adequately explain my need to be touched without sounding like a sissy. Furthermore, I feared the rejection that would likely follow such a bizarre request for help." One man put it well when he said, "As a gay man, I've found it's easier for me to get sex on the streets than to get a hug in church."

There are many people in my life, even now, whom I've dreamed of wrapping my arms around, but I don't dare try because I believe it would make them uncomfortable and because I fear their rejection.

Make yourself uncomfortable.

If you're not sure how to hug someone who is struggling with homosexuality, just open your arms. If they need your touch, they'll walk right in. Allowing someone who has struggled with homosexuality to get close to you is the greatest gift you can give them. Whether this takes the form of touch, talk, or even something as cliche as going to a movie. Learn their love language and then speak it.

Randy Newman writes, "For far too many [homosexual strugglers], a crucial missing ingredient in the healing process is friendship with a heterosexual Christian who will accept them, pray with them, and embrace them."

Surrogacy

As I mentioned earlier, homosexual activity is often an unconscious attempt to recover the same-sex parent's love through sexual intimacy with a member of one's gender. Richard Cohen writes, "Today significant emphasis is placed on sexual identity and sexual behavior. One primary cause of this preoccupation is the lack of intimacy within the family. The pursuit of sex then becomes a substitute for [parents'] love."

The best way to eliminate the need for a substitute is to get the real thing. Those wishing to overcome same-sex attractions should make every effort to reconcile with their parents if those relationships have ever been compromised. Some of us have experienced abuse, neglect, and other forms of rejection from our parents, but harboring bitterness only fuels our homosexual desires by emphasizing the disconnection that took place. One ex-gay man put it very well: "If you want to experience victory over your homosexual attractions, forgive your parents."

Often one must work through unimaginable amounts of anger toward mom or dad for any injustices they may have committed. Because one's inability to identify with his or her gender is often connected to one's inability to express anger during the formative years, expression of anger toward mom or dad as an adult can be an important healing tool. As Nicolosi has said, "Anger is a link to our true identity." Furthermore, if the anger is released constructively, it should make it easier for the struggler to forgive mom and dad for not providing what was needed in order to facilitate heterosexual development.

It should be noted that parents are not always to blame for the homosexuality of their children. However, the struggler will likely still need to express anger, and the parents should allow it. (For more information on the expression of anger as it relates to homosexuality, see chapter 19 of Dr. Joseph Nicolosi's book *Reparative Therapy of Male Homosexuality*.)

The disconnection that occurs between a child and his or her same-gender parent while growing up is often what facilitates the disconnection that takes place between a child and his or her gender as a whole. Therefore, reconciling with one's parents can open one up to reconciliation with one's gender.

The proper processing of unresolved anger, followed by the forgiving of past hurts inflicted by mom or dad, will free the homosexual struggler to receive the love and affirmation of their parents that they need in order to facilitate this reconciliation, assuming mom and dad are willing to give it. All children need affirmation from their parents. The importance of affirmation can even be seen at the beginning of Christ's earthly ministry. In Matthew 3, we can see how Jesus received affirmation from his father before he began his ministry: "And when Jesus had been baptized, just as he came up from the water, suddenly the heavens were opened to him and he saw the Spirit of God descending like a dove and alighting on him. And a voice from heaven said, 'This is my Son, the Beloved, with whom I am well pleased'" (vv. 16–17).

Lenny Carluzzi writes, "This observation cannot be minimized. For the Father to say, 'This is my Son,' was to say to Jesus, 'You belong to me, I can see Me in you, you are part of Me.' Oh how these words would correct the course of a young sensitive boy who seeks to belong to his father, who is searching for his identity as a man, and belonging with his peers."

For those of us whose parents may be unable or unwilling to help us through the process of gender reconciliation, we must complete it through a surrogate (substitute parent). Mona Riley writes, "When children become insecure in [their identity], their blocked, God-given longing to enter fully into their gender identity may begin to express itself in longings to bond with a substitute parent."

This was the case in my life. As I mentioned in chapter 1, I found my surrogate father at an Italian restaurant in Chicago about five years prior to the publishing of this book. He changed my life.

The concept of surrogacy can also be used to prevent the development of homosexuality in children who have lost a parent. No child should be left behind.

The ramifications of this concept extend far beyond sexual development. If a child is missing either a father or a mother, it is the job of the church to fill this gap in the child's life (Matt. 12:46–50). This will ensure not only healthy sexual development but also healthy emotional and spiritual development as well. Riley writes, "God designed His creation to work together in harmony. The larger community should provide solid and secure relationships to augment those of the family unit. Older women should teach and mentor younger women and girls, encouraging them in feminine character and strength. Older men should teach and mentor younger men and boys, promoting masculine vision and responsibility."

The process of surrogate intervention can be further helped through the therapeutic process known as reparative therapy. As I mentioned in chapter 5, there are many psychotherapists successfully treating homosexuals today. Because these therapists understand the issues facing the homosexual struggler, they often serve as the perfect surrogates. According to Dr. Nicolosi, "In a relationship with a same-sex therapist, a client can find some of what he missed in the failed father-son bond." This concept applies to females as well. (For a list of psychotherapists trained in this area, contact the National Association of Research and Therapy of Homosexuality. Their website is www.NARTH.com.)

Although surrogacy is vital for those whose homosexuality resulted from a lack of bonding with one or more of their parents, certainly not every occurrence of homosexuality has to do with one's parents. I know some homosexually oriented people who had very healthy relationships with their parents while growing up. For them, the process of gender disconnection may have taken place between them and their same-gender peers. In these cases, an individual's reconciliation to his or her gender is begun by reconciling with his or her same-gender peers. This is where camaraderie comes in.

Camaraderie

Many men who struggle with homosexuality remember an inability to connect with their male peers during their formative years. One of Dr. Nicolosi's clients reported having a dream about a male coworker with whom he desired friendship. The client's dream illustrated his residual need to connect with his male peers: "I was an adult, but I was playing like a little boy, and I was on roller skates, carrying a red toy truck under my arm, on my way to this coworker's house. There I stood, outside his house, waiting for him to come out to play with me."

In his book *Take Off the Masks*, Malcolm Boyd talks about an experience he had as an adolescent: "On one occasion I visited a house where I saw two men, wearing only their shorts, seated in a bedroom. Their easy camaraderie, with a sense of male secrets shared and easy body contact between them, made me feel like an outsider. Had I missed an initiation into maleness?"

During my adolescence, I felt like I was always on the outside looking in, watching as other boys connected with each other but somehow unable to figure out for myself how in the world they were doing it. I felt as though I had missed this "initiation into maleness."

One of the ways I have recovered this initiation and reconciled with my gender is through camaraderie with my peers. Often the men through whom I experience the most healing are those in whom I see characteristics that represent masculinity to me. These characteristics are often the very qualities I am searching for in myself, qualities that I may initially be attracted to in an erotic sense. According to E. Kaplan, "It seems apparent that some homosexuals choose as sexual objects people who have characteristics–physical, personal or both–in which they themselves feel deficient."

F. Weiss writes, "The [sexual] partner is often the externalized symbol of the lost, repressed part of his own self, for example, his 'masculinity.'"

Although I may initially feel a sexual attraction, because I have refrained from sexual activity, I have learned to internalize these relationships in a nonsexual way. Even casual relationships with guys who represent masculinity to me have allowed me to be initiated into, or reconciled with, my gender. In fact, I've learned to internalize even the subtlest forms of masculine affirmation, such as being asked by a male peer to sit next to him on the bus or being invited to tour a German castle with him.

A few years ago, I took a self-guided tour of a castle in Germany with a group of friends from my church. I remember going first into the dungeon just to see what was in there, and one of the guys from my church group, Dave, wandered in there with me. Even after I could tell that Dave was done looking at the dungeon, he just stood there for a minute next to me. At first I wondered, *Why is he just standing there?* But then I realized he was waiting for me. We were going to walk around the castle *together.*

After a lifetime of being rejected by my male peers, the realization that Dave had accepted me was almost too joyous for words, yet I refrained from doing the jig my heart wanted me to do and calmly toured the castle with Dave by my side, internalizing every precious moment of desperately needed masculine affirmation.

The night before writing this chapter, I attended a Valentine's Day party with some friends from church. The party was unique from other parties I've been to in that it was organized entirely by the guys in my church. The purpose was to do something nice for the girls on Valentine's Day.

There was a clear distinction between the role the guys played and the role the girls played. The girls were all seated at tables, while the guys made their way back and forth between the kitchen and the dining room catering to their every whim. The camaraderie that was fostered among "the guys" as we created and served the meal that night created within me a genuine sense of belonging to my gender.

On my way out, I came up behind two close friends, Pete and Steve, and propped my arms up on their shoulders just long enough to say "hi." They each responded by touching their hands to my back just for an instant, as if to say, "Yeah, you're one of us." To them, it was a natural response to my social cue, but to me, it was a powerful healing tool.

Another way that I have achieved camaraderie with my peers is through my ability to perceive similarities between them and myself. Often during small-group sessions at church, guys will get together to discuss our struggles and our victories. Many of the things we share are similar, and I find myself thinking, "Oh, he struggles with that too. He's just like me!" When I see aspects of my personality in other males, it's like my own masculinity finds a harbor.

Men who have never struggled with homosexuality are also aware of their need for camaraderie with other men, as has been evidenced by the growing men's movement in our culture. Even Christian author John Eldredge has written about the importance of healthy same-sex relationships:

> So much healing took place in my life simply through my friendship with Brent. We were [work] partners, but far more than that, we were friends. We spent hours together fly-fishing, backpacking, hanging out in pubs. Just spending time with a man I truly respected, a real man who loved and respected me–nothing heals quite like that. At first I feared that I was fooling him, that he'd see right through it any day and drop me. But he didn't, and what happened instead was validation. My heart knew that if a man I know is a man thinks I'm one, too, well then, maybe I am one after all.

Forming Relationships

For females, camaraderie can be initiated through mutual interests such as scrap-booking, knitting, or even getting together to watch a "chick flick." Most females don't require an activity in order to establish a friendship. Males, however, are a different story.

Although I have many male friends whom I can just sit down and enjoy a cup of coffee with, there are many whom it seems I can connect with only during the course of some activity. According to Dr. Nicolosi, this is the more common means of connection in male friendships: "Male bonding characteristically occurs through a shared physical activity or common task. Unlike women, who can sit face-to-face and disclose directly, men bond indirectly through a shared doing. It is this bonding that fosters male identification."

For many male strugglers, learning to participate in a sport such as football or even golf has helped them to form relationships with their male peers. If a male struggler is afraid of sports, I would certainly encourage him to give it a try, not only because it can be a tool to help him connect to other guys but also because physical exertion can put one in touch with his masculinity. However, as far as male relationships are concerned, one does not *have* to enjoy sports in order to connect with other guys.

Relationships can be formed through participation in any common task or shared interest, such as music or technology. One can even start a friendship through something as shallow as a mutually appreciated movie or amusement park ride. But in order to find a common interest, the struggler must put himself in social situations with other guys. Joe Dallas describes the next step in creating male friendships: "You look for men within the group who seem friendly and receptive to you. That's not too hard; just keep your eyes open and, as Solomon said, show yourself to be friendly. When the door to conversation seems open, pursue it. If you're shy, as many strugglers are, you may experience a thousand anxieties at this point. But keep in mind the fact that nobody can see those anxieties but you, so don't let them stop you. As you gradually gain acceptance and sense a desire on another man's part to know you better, follow through."

There really are no hard and fast rules when it comes to connecting with guys. If a guy makes himself interesting, other guys will want to be his friend. For what it's worth, I have almost no interest in sports whatsoever, but I have started many friendships with the guys in my church just by making jokes about the food that we eat when we're together. I have been labeled "the health-food guy" because I am always talking, in a tongue-in-cheek manner, about the nutritional consequences of fat, sugar, and preservatives.

If you are not involved in a church, I strongly recommend that you find one. Never underestimate the power of a healthy, God-fearing church body to give strugglers the support they need to overcome homosexual attractions. Jeff Konrad talks about the support he received from his church after he decided to leave behind his homosexuality: "I ached physically from all the emotional turmoil. But several Christian heterosexual men made themselves available any time of the day or night. I'm alive today because those guys loved me."

As I mentioned in chapter 2, because homosexual strugglers often have a hard time connecting with their same-gender peers, some churches have started mentoring programs in which heterosexuals are paired with homosexual strugglers. This can greatly reduce the burden placed on the homosexual struggler as he or she seeks to find a place in the world of men or women, respectively.

All of the things mentioned in this section can help a struggler foster camaraderie with his or her same-gender peers, and just like with touch, the proper internalization of masculine affirmation through camaraderie will extinguish homosexual attractions. Dr. Nicolosi writes, "Homosexual clients report that when they begin to know another man intimately, their sexual interest in him diminishes. It is always, they report, the distant person who is sexually attractive."

It's important to note that if the struggler is establishing nonsexual relationships with same-gender peers for the first time, it is likely that some issues will surface that he or she may need some help to process. These could include feelings of jealousy, inferiority, inadequacy, codependency, self-condemnation, and misplaced anger. The homosexual struggler may also have to work at not idolizing his or her same-gender friends; the goal is to relate to members of one's gender as an equal. This requires the struggler to be assertive and to take risks in the relationship by honestly disclosing his or her feelings and trusting that the person will still be there for them in friendship. According to Dr. Nicolosi, "[The struggler] is challenged to overcome feelings of unworthiness and self-condemnation. Gradually he will learn how to show vulnerability and ask for help, and to be transparent and receptive to the lessons other men can teach him." (The same could be said for females.)

For me, the ability to show vulnerability around my male peers has been particularly significant to my progress in overcoming homosexuality. While I am careful to give my friends at least a few months to get to know me before I disclose any information about my struggle, deciding which friends to tell has been mostly a matter of prayer. Telling the wrong person could result in devastating rejection. However, without exception, every single guy I've told about my struggle has been supportive and caring.

A struggler's ability to disclose his or her homosexual problem to his or her same-sex peers is significant because it creates an added intimacy in the relationship, and because it fosters a sense of security: "They know this about me, and they still love me!" It's also important because it opens the door for the struggler to request further help when needed: "I'm feeling very disconnected today; I think I need a hug."

All three of the healing mechanisms I have discussed in this chapter–nonsexual touch, surrogacy, and camaraderie–have been crucial to my healing process because they all facilitate the retrieval of gender identification. My inability to identify with my father while growing up created a disconnection between me and my masculinity. But as I have illustrated in this chapter, I have found that it's never too late to recover the gender identification I missed out on as a child and, in doing so, to learn to view men as friends instead of lovers.

The Invitation to a Man's World

It should also be noted that, for men, connecting with the masculine can also be facilitated by connecting with the *dangerous.* John Eldredge points out a perfect illustration of this concept in the movie *A Perfect World.* Kevin Costner plays an escaped convict named Butch Haynes who kidnaps a fatherless little boy named Phillip and then hits the road. During the trip, Butch and Phillip end up bonding, and Butch actually develops a fatherly attachment to the boy. When Butch finds out that Phillip has never ridden on a roller coaster, he is enraged. As a result, Butch ends up strapping the little boy to the top of his vehicle so he can discover what true adventure is like. Eldredge comments, "That's the invitation into a man's world, a world involving danger."

While working at a wilderness camp in Colorado one summer, my friends and I accepted this invitation almost daily. We climbed through mysterious caves in the dark, slid down glaciers nestled against jagged mountainsides, battled fatigue on hikes that sometimes seemed to last for days, and twice during the summer we found ourselves at the top of a huge mountain in the middle of a massive lightning storm! Realizing that I had it in me to meet these challenges was a powerful affirmation of my masculinity. This was an especially unique form of affirmation because it came not from other men *but from the mountains*. They asked me if I have what it takes to be a man, and I answered them.

Watching God Work

It has been interesting to watch God facilitate my healing process as he continues to put people in my life to provide the "stream" of masculine affirmation I need in order to grow. During high school, I worked at a Christian radio station. I received many phone calls from lonely people who listened to the station and, hearing my friendly voice over the air, decided they wanted to hear it over the phone too.

One such caller was a fourteen-year-old boy named Andy. Because I had experienced rejection from nearly all of my male peers in high school, I had an intense desire to be affirmed by males who were my age. Andy's phone calls provided a constant stream of male affirmation that not only kept me from seeking a sexual form of male attention elsewhere but also played a pivotal role in reconciling me with my gender.

Even now, though Andy and I have both moved on to other things, I can see how every relationship God has put in my life has served a purpose in my process of change, as well as provided for the healing of the wounds of my past. Dave is a great example. The affirmation he provides is powerful and consistent. Every time I see him, without fail, he looks me right in the eye and flashes one of the biggest, most beautiful smiles known to man. On some occasions, he doesn't even have anything to say, but the smile still comes, and each time it does, I experience healing.

Andy's presence in my life during high school was not an accident, and neither is Dave's now. God is orchestrating the fulfillment of my need to be affirmed by members of my gender and, in so doing, is orchestrating the emergence of heterosexual attractions.

The most powerful healing agent in my life has been the presence of real live men who have offered me the nonsexual and nonromantic love I've needed; they are my brothers. These relationships have meant the world to me; they nurture my soul. Like a light in an underground tunnel, they provide a path of escape from the prison of disconnection and abandonment. It's a prison that I still remember, although the memory fades a little more each time one of these guys opens his arms.

And I walk right in.

In summary, individuals who desire change must experience love from their parents, their same-sex peers, and their God. For me, the process of achieving freedom from homosexual desires has come not from any one method but from a combination of healing agents perfectly orchestrated by my creator, who loves me (Rom. 8:28). Although there is a body of purely scientific data that secular researchers have used to treat people with unwanted homosexual desires, I've been told by some who are involved in this work that to undergo the process of change using any method that does not include fervent, personal prayer is useless.

Still Skeptical?

I have spoken with some homosexuals who insist that the causes of homosexuality that I've outlined do not apply to them. They claim to have had healthy relationships with their same-gender parents and peers while growing up. Therefore, they conclude that my theories are bogus. However, because many of the relational deficits that contribute to homosexual development are unconscious, it's possible that, for some of these people, relational issues with same-gender parents or peers are present but suppressed. This is where counseling can help. Joe Dallas writes, "I've found, without exception, that when the [homosexual] fulfills his responsibility to abstain from homosexual actions and is ready to look at the nonsexual parts of his life needing correction, unfinished business with others invariably shows up." Once the emotional deficit that caused the homosexuality is identified and allowed to surface, nonerotic affirmation from one's parents, peers, or surrogates can be properly internalized.

Some in the gay community have tried to discredit professionals who offer help to those desiring to change their sexual orientation by suggesting that such therapy is provoking their clientele to commit suicide. However, there is absolutely no evidence to support this claim. According to Dr. Nicolosi, "I've been doing this work for almost twenty years, treating men and women with unwanted homosexuality. For all twenty years, I've been accused of causing my clients to commit suicide, yet I've never once had a client commit suicide or even attempt suicide."

Others have criticized reparative therapy and other change methods by claiming that any study that has ever been done to measure their rate of success is "outdated" and has since been "debunked." Former homosexual Ben Newman wrote this in his rebuttal to a recent book called *Anything but Straight*, which denigrates orientational change:

> For as many times as [Wayne] Besen [attacks sexual reorientation] throughout his book, you would think he would provide some evidence. He repeatedly labels reparative therapy principles and research as "old, outdated ideas." . . . Yet Besen offers virtually nothing in the way of evidence that the research and principles supporting reparative therapy have actually been disproved or discredited.
>
> He claims that findings from Dr. Irving Bieber's 1962 study of 106 homosexual clients (which found, for instance, that all 106 men experienced profound disturbance in their relation-

> ship with their fathers) "could not be replicated and were disproved by more diligent researchers." But Besen doesn't offer so much as a footnote to support this claim. . . .
>
> In contrast, in his seminal work, *Reparative Therapy of Male Homosexuality: A New Clinical Approach* (1991), Dr. Joseph Nicolosi references no fewer than 300 books, academic studies and journal articles as he lays out the core principles of reparative therapy.

Newman concludes, "Reparative therapy has not been discredited. It has simply fallen out of favor since the 1973 vote by the board of the American Psychiatric Association to remove homosexuality from its official encyclopedia of mental disorders. . . . The research hasn't been disproved; it has simply been disenfranchised by the political correctness of the times."

Psychological journals have published peer-reviewed scientific studies in the past few years that report significant success among individuals wishing to change from gay to straight. In fact, more than fifty years of research on the subject has produced data and published accounts documenting easily more than three thousand cases of change from homosexual to heterosexual attraction and functioning.

Similarly, a self-report survey was conducted among more than 850 individuals and 200 therapists and counselors. Preliminary findings revealed that before counseling or therapy, 68 percent of the respondents perceived themselves as exclusively or almost entirely homosexual, while only 13 percent identified themselves as such after counseling or therapy. Data was tabulated by statisticians at Brigham Young University.

Dr. Robert Spitzer, the psychiatrist who led the charge to take homosexuality out of the American Psychiatric Association's list of mental disorders, conducted a study to find out if homosexuals really could change their orientation. Many of the participants in Dr. Spitzer's study experienced a marked increase in both the frequency and satisfaction of heterosexual activity, while those in marital relationships noted more emotional fulfillment between their spouses and themselves. Respondents were required to have experienced such benefits for a period of five years or more.

Spitzer still believes that homosexuality is not technically a mental illness, and I agree, but he also believes that gays can change. Spitzer said that his study "clearly goes beyond anecdotal information and provides evidence that reparative therapy is sometimes successful." Dr. Spitzer's study was published in the *Archives of Sexual Behavior* just as I was finishing this book. In addition, Dr. Warren Throckmorton has published ex-gay research in the APA's prestigious journal *Professional Psychology: Research and Practice.* This is just a sampling of the scientific evidence that is available to support the effectiveness of sexual reorientation.

One of the most common questions I am asked is, "Do ex-gays really change their orientation, or is it just behavior modification?" The answer is, "Both." Just like many aspects of life, if you change the behavior first, the feelings will follow. This requires the homosexual struggler to discipline himself or herself to view their same-sex counterparts as friends, rather than lovers. As I mentioned earlier in this chapter, if I meet an attractive guy, I can choose to focus on his personality instead of his body. In time, even the desire to focus on his body will disappear.

An excellent illustration of this concept is found in the movie *A Beautiful Mind.* Russell Crowe plays the role of John Nash, a mathematics professor who battles schizophrenic hallucinations. Imaginary characters follow him everywhere he goes, tormenting him with mindless tasks and emotionally draining insults. For most of the movie, he is enslaved by them, carrying out their every demand. Toward the end of the movie, however, he starts learning how to ignore them, and as he does, they get quieter and quieter.

In the last scene of the movie Nash walks down a hallway, hand in hand with his wife. In the background, all of his imaginary friends stand in the corner of the room, completely silent. He wasn't even being tempted by them anymore. So it is for those who struggle with same-sex attractions.

After just one year of therapy, a client of Dr. Nicolosi's reported, "What my homosexual feelings used to be, they aren't now. They're still around, they're still there, but they're not as upsetting. The improvement is in how they affect me emotionally . . . how much I am preoccupied by them."

Another client said, "Now those homosexual fantasies are more like a gnat buzzing around my ear." Although there was a time when I wondered if being ex-gay would involve only a change in behavior, I have been amazed at some of the reactions I have had toward females in the past few years. As time goes by, I am becoming more and more attracted to women and less and less physically attracted to men.

There is a distinction between God's kind of love (the Greek term is "agape" love) and the world's kind of love. God's love begins with our will and ends with our emotions, while the world's love begins with the emotions and ends with the will.

Another common question, though usually framed as an accusation from those looking to discount my message, is, "How do I know I'm not just bisexual and have chosen to enjoy my other side for a while?"

A scientific survey published in the journal *Psychological Reports* found that of 318 subjects who described themselves as *exclusively* homosexual (not bisexual), 45.4 percent reported having made major shifts in their sexual orientation. (These individuals also reported significant improvements in their psychological, interpersonal, and spiritual well-being.)

Furthermore, if ex-gays really are all bisexuals choosing to "enjoy our other side," why did so many of us spend decades of our lives attracted exclusively to our own sex and didn't experience any opposite-sex attractions until we engaged in an intentional effort to change our sexual orientation? Maybe it is only coincidence. Or maybe all of us ex-gays are just playing mental gymnastics to convince ourselves that we changed. When the rubber meets the road, opponents of change will always find a reason to believe that people like me are fakes if that's what they really want to believe. And that is their right.

But not all gay activists fit this mold. Camille Paglia, a self-identified lesbian and atheist, writes, “Is gay identity so fragile that it cannot bear the thought that some people may not wish to be gay? . . . Sexuality is highly fluid, and reversals are theoretically possible. However, habit is refractory, once the sensory pathways have been blazed and deepened by repetition–a phenomenon obvious in the struggle with obesity, smoking, alcoholism, or drug addiction. . . . Helping gays learn how to function heterosexually, if they so wish, is a perfectly worthy aim.”

Prevention

Now that you know how to overcome homosexual attractions, I feel it’s necessary to spend at least a few paragraphs on the subject of prevention. A father can reduce the likelihood of his son’s developing homosexual attractions by

- being patient with him, reassuring him that mistakes are a natural part of life.
- letting him know when he sees characteristics of himself in his son.
- doing things with him regularly.
- showing him affection freely. This includes verbal affirmation and physical affirmation such as wrestling and hugging.
- helping him identify his interests, whether it’s a sport or an artistic talent.

- encouraging him to develop healthy relationships with other boys his age during the preteen years.
- recognizing areas in which he may be lacking social skills and teaching him to compensate.
- encouraging him to freely express his emotions and feelings without consequences or verbal put-downs.
- modeling a healthy and affectionate relationship with his mother, which includes speaking favorably of her even when she is not around.
- not shying away from getting undressed with or showering with him. This will reduce the potential that he will develop an unnatural curiosity toward the male body.
- maintaining close male friendships so that his son can see him interacting with other men in healthy ways.
- encouraging gender-conforming behavior while gently steering him away from gender nonconforming behavior. (It's okay for a boy to play with Barbie for a little while, but he should be given a gentle "nudge" in the direction of the Ninja Turtles or G.I. Joe.)

Furthermore, when a boy is afraid to try something new, his father should encourage him to face his fear, and he should stand beside him as he does so. Mothers can prevent their daughters from becoming homosexual through many of the same techniques described above, as well as by promoting a healthy relationship between her and her father. (For more information on preventing homosexuality, see the resources section.)

To the Struggler

If you are engaged in the struggle to overcome homosexual feelings, I hope the information in this chapter helps you get in touch with the unmet needs that are driving your attractions and has motivated you to ask for the help you need. Now that you know what you are really after when you pursue homosexual relationships, you can't go back to them. You know too much. As Dr. Nicolosi writes, "Insight and self-awareness unavoidably alter the erotic illusion. Like a theatre patron who witnesses a prop fall during a scene in a play, he can never see the scene in the same illusional way."

As I mentioned in chapter 1, most people who have given up on changing their sexual orientation, convinced that it can't be done, likely have done so because they were given an inaccurate or incomplete explanation of what the process entails.

During the question and answer time at the end of one of my seminars, a man raised his hand to tell me that he had "lived a lie" for twenty years while married to a woman and would no longer entertain even the slightest hope for change. "I tried for *twenty* years," he said. "Nothing ever changed."

But when I asked him what methods he had tried in order to facilitate a change, he quietly responded that he had done absolutely nothing. He just expected that if he stayed married long enough, change would happen on its own. There is some truth to his reasoning, since behavior is a powerful conditioning tool, but it must be coupled with the other tools I have described in this chapter. The desire to bond sexually with someone of the opposite sex can come only after the process of bonding nonsexually with members of one's own gender is completed.

On the other hand, you may be reading this as someone who has done many of the things mentioned in this chapter and is still experiencing attractions to members of your gender. You've probably said things like, "When will I change? When will the temptation end? When will the sexual attraction toward people of my own sex end and the attraction for the opposite sex begin? I thought God promised me freedom. This whole thing is a crock! I'll never change."

I believe that there are two bedrock beliefs upon which a person's success in reorienting their sexuality depends. The first has to do with identity. Neil Anderson says that a person cannot consistently behave in a way that's different from the way in which they see or think about themselves. Do you see yourself as a homosexual or a heterosexual? This may sound corny, but it's actually one of the most powerful tools at your disposal.

During the early stages of my struggle with homosexuality, it seemed as though every voice in society was trying to tell me who I was. Some said, "You're gay; embrace it!" while others said, "You're a fag; you deserve to die." In some cases, it seemed like the voices were simply saying, "You'll never know who you are."

Those weren't the only voices though. There was actually one more, a much softer voice. It said, "I know exactly who you are, because it's who I created you to be." The knowledge that I am, in fact, a heterosexual created in me the determination to go forward even when it seemed like there was no hope.

The second belief has to do with how a person sees God. In the Old Testament book of Jeremiah, God makes a promise to a group of his followers who had been taken captive by the rulers of Babylon. If they would seek him wholeheartedly, God would rescue them from captivity:

> For surely I know the plans I have for you, says the LORD, plans for your welfare and not for harm, to give you a future with hope. Then when you call upon me and come and pray to me, I will hear you. When you search for me, you will find me; if you seek me with all your heart, I will let you find me, says the LORD, and I will restore your fortunes and gather you from all the nations and all the places where I have driven you, says the LORD, and I will bring you back to the place from which I sent you into exile. (29:11–14)

God made them an amazing promise, and he came through for them. What's interesting about this story is that it's a perfect summary of God's relating to humankind throughout the ages. It's the story of God's *coming through for* his creation. Consider the story of Abraham and Sarah. God promised Abraham that his descendants would be "as numerous as the stars in the sky." The only problem? Sarah was barren! But because Abraham believed God's promise, despite the apparent impossibility of the task, God gave Abraham a son named Isaac, through whom God birthed the nation of Israel.

These stories are important for two reasons. First, they affirm the nature of a God who can be counted on. But more than that, they reveal the nature of a God who *must* be counted on, as the beneficiaries in both of these stories received the fruit of God's promises only because they believed them to be true.

Second, these stories affirm the character of a God who must be waited for. Read the whole story behind these two examples and you'll find that Babylon's captives had to wait seventy years for their freedom, and Abraham didn't get Isaac until he was a hundred years old. A person can enjoy relationship with God at any time, but the promises of God are often slow in coming. Nonetheless, if you believe them, they are coming.

I know dozens of men and women who have successfully changed their sexual orientation, regardless of their initial fear that it couldn't be done. If you observed their lives, you'd never guess that they used to be gay. Most of them have fulfilling relationships with their spouses, including sexually, while some of them are content just being celibate. But for many of these men and women, sexual reorientation was not necessarily their main objective. Their objective, instead, was obedience to God's plan for their lives. In other words, they were not anxiously waiting for God to align their feelings with their behavior; rather, they had already committed to live heterosexual lives *regardless of their feelings*. It is this kind of commitment through which God works best.

In summary, those who change have one thing in common: perseverance. The process of change takes time because it rides on the sanctification process, which is a lifelong process. And Jesus, being the facilitator of our sanctification (or "spiritual cleansing"), is ultimately in charge of the results.

Proverbs 24:16 (NASB) says, "For a righteous man falls seven times, and rises again." So it is with those who are working to overcome unwanted homosexual attractions. But a genuine desire to change, coupled with a spirit of prayer and a strong support system, can overcome all obstacles.

It certainly did for me, and it all started because one man loved me enough to open his arms.

And I walked right in.

Afterword

Why Can't I Be Proud?

A call for ex-gay people to come out of our own closets

Let the redeemed of the LORD say so.

–Psalm 107:2

The multicolored banner filled up the sky in front of Iowa's state capitol. Floats occupied by homosexuals, transvestites, and sadomasochists were lined up, engines running as they waited for their cue. It was the third time I had attended the event, bringing with me a table, a cooler, some bottled water, and about a half-dozen friends. Our only goal was to show love to a group of people who, before we came, had probably perceived only hatred from those who claimed to represent Jesus.

As attendees of that year's gay-pride celebration walked by our table, we offered them a bottle of water, some friendly conversation, and a 4 x 5 card with the web address and phone number of a man who had walked away from homosexuality many years ago. For the most part, the people at the celebration treated us with respect, even after reading the card. However, one man, after engaging us in a friendly discussion about his background, walked off in haste upon finding out why we were there. He refused to take our water or our literature.

What about our culture makes it politically correct to celebrate the lives of those who identify themselves as lesbian, gay, bisexual, or transgender, yet, like the man at the parade, turn our backs in shame even at the idea that someone might choose to find happiness outside the gay life?

Why can't I be proud to be an ex-gay?

In 2001, when Dr. Robert Spitzer started studying whether homosexuals really could change their orientation, much of secular psychiatry shunned him, and gay psychiatry flat out lambasted him. The most prevalent accusation was that his study was invalid because he got almost all of his subjects from religious organizations, and those people were seeking help only because "the Bible told them to" (1 Cor. 6:9–11), not because they genuinely desired to be heterosexual.

Many people who were prominent voices in the media at that time also blew off Dr. Spitzer's "conversion," and for the same reason. (The real reason those seeking help for their homosexuality seek it from the church is that most secular psychologists have turned their backs on us.)

This is just one example of the media's blatant refusal, even in the face of powerful evidence, to acknowledge or substantiate the lives of those who have embraced what Spitzer calls our "heterosexual potential." The media's efforts at demonizing those who have changed from homosexual to heterosexual have contributed significantly to the silence of those of us who have walked away from homosexuality.

The voice of a hostile media, coupled with the fear of rejection from friends and family, keeps many of us in our *own* closets. In addition, we have been taught to avoid others who struggle as we do. We have been protected by anonymity in religious programs and support groups that meet in rooms with unmarked doors. Why are we so ashamed? Although much of my adolescence felt like pure hell as I worked to make sense of my homosexual feelings, now that I'm approaching the other side of that struggle, I feel pretty darn proud of myself–and of God for the work he's done in me.

It says in 2 Timothy 1:7 that God has given us a spirit not of timidity but of power, yet many ex-gays cower in fear at the thought that someone might find out they used to be gay. I understand why many former homosexuals don't want to "come out" as ex-gays. We *used* to be gay; we're not anymore, so there's really nothing to "come out" about. Furthermore, many of us have legitimate concerns about the welfare of our families and our careers.

Some ex-gays don't feel led to share their story with others as I do, and that's okay. I do not condemn them. But I believe that many of us who could or should speak up don't, and because we don't, the world is left wondering if gays really can change. They wonder if ex-gays are really an integral part of society, or if our population is confined to a few activists who work for conservative special-interest groups, since it often seems those are the only ones willing to tell their story.

I believe the most powerful tool we have to garner acceptance of ourselves and our ideas is personal transparency before people whom we come in contact with daily. Consider how homosexuals have benefited from this strategy. A decade or so ago, when most of society was repulsed by homosexuality, few homosexuals were willing to identify themselves as such, and for good reason. They likely would have been ostracized. But after the Stonewall riot of 1969, when LGBT people had finally had enough, many began identifying themselves, regardless of the cost.

During the same period, our society's attitude toward homosexuality began to shift. Why? Because most people who detested homosexuality did so only because, to them, it was just an abstract idea, a behavior. Something that's "out there." But as soon as they met an actual human being who was gay, it became personal. Their acceptance of the *person* who revealed their homosexuality shifted to acceptance of the *concept* of homosexuality in general.

As Mel White writes, "All the studies prove that people who know personally a gay man or lesbian are the people who stand for justice on our behalf. People who do not know personally (or who don't think they know) a lesbian or gay are those who are more likely to vote against us. Coming out, stating proudly who we are to the people we know and love, has become the first and most important step we take on the road to doing justice."

Many of the LGBT people who attended my seminar in western Iowa had a poor image of ex-gay people, likely because the only knowledge they had about us is what they had read in pro-gay publications, which usually paint ex-gays as "freaks." But when they met me and found that I was just like them in many ways, many shifted their view of ex-gays. In chapter 2, I shared a quote from a gay man who attended one of Inqueery's seminars. He said, "After sitting through your presentation, I was immediately reminded that I needed to be less judgmental of people who self-identify as 'ex-gay,' especially when they, like you, speak out against discrimination and prejudice based on sexual orientation. Until you, I just hadn't met an ex-gay person who was not openly heterosexist and homophobic."

It says in Psalm 107 that the redeemed of the Lord should say so. It's time for those of us who have changed from gay to straight to crawl out from under our rocks and start "saying so" about the change that God has made in us. This will begin the process of changing society's views of ex-gays. It will also provide individuals who are questioning their sexuality with the information they need to make an informed decision about their future, especially young people, who are often mistakenly told that one homosexual experience must define their sexuality for a lifetime.

In conclusion, while it's still hard to be gay in America, it is getting easier. Society is learning that LGBT people can be really cool people and have made many significant contributions to our society. But to be ex-gay in America today is very difficult. While I think that LGBT people get sick and tired of hearing straight people tell them that they are supposed to change, it's also very difficult for people like me to hear LGBT people tell me that I don't exist, that change is impossible.

Change *is* possible. And it's time that those of us who have changed start to "say so."

Notes

Introduction

9 . . . *they have met a Christian.* Tim Wilkins, "I Still Love Homosexuals (part 1)," www.crossministry.org.

10 . . . *love thy neighbor.* "Your Story," www.anotherway.com.

11 . . . *a place of safety? Why Christians Need to Get Involved,* VHS (Colorado Springs: Focus on the Family, 1996).

Chapter 1: My Story

24 . . . *I find incredibly unethical.* "Narth's Response to 'Just the Facts about Sexual Orientation and Youth,'" www.Narth.com.

24 . . . *I started to change.* Ibid.

25 . . . *to see myself differently.* Ibid.

25 . . . *client who seeks it.* Joseph Nicolosi, *Reparative Therapy of Male Homosexuality* (Northvale, NJ: Aronson Books, 1997), 20.

Chapter 2: Whoever Loves First

33 . . . *myself would stay intact.* Joe Dallas, *A Strong Delusion* (Eugene, OR: Harvest House, 1996), 133–4.

38 . . . *that they were sinners.* Ken Ham, *Why Won't They Listen?* (Green Forest, AZ: Master Books, 2002), 39–47.

41 . . . *was the whole point.* Steve Bush, *Dominating Other Cultures,* compact disc (self-published, 2002). The quote is paraphrased from the CD.

43 . . . *touch first base first!* Don Richardson, *Eternity in Their Hearts* (Ventura, CA: Regal Books, 1981), 21.

43 . . . *TO AN UNKNOWN GOD.* Ibid., 21.

46 . . . *training they had received.* Ibid., 23.

47 . . . *talk about his homosexuality.* Randy Newman, "When Your Friend Says, 'I'm Gay'" *Discipleship Journal* 138 (November–December 2003), 33.

49 . . . *to communicate with them.* Ham, *Why Won't They Listen?* 36.

50 . . . *than heterosexuals molest children.* Timothy Dailey, "Homosexuality and Child Sexual Abuse," www.FRC.org.

50 . . . *homosexuals are not pedophiles.* Jeffrey Satinover, M.D., *Homosexuality and the Politics of Truth* (Grand Rapids: Baker, 1996), 62.

52 . . . *described in the Bible.* Jerry Arterburn, *How Will I Tell My Mother?* (Nashville: Oliver Nelson, 1988), 120–21.

53 . . . *him for many years.* Philip Yancey, *The Jesus I Never Knew* (Grand Rapids: Zondervan, 1995), 171.

55 . . . *prevalent among homosexuals,* D. McWhirter and A. Madison, *The Male Couple: How Relationships Develop* (Englewood Cliffs, NJ: Prentice-Hall, 1984). The writers surveyed 156 gay couples and found that only seven had been able to maintain sexual fidelity.

55 . . . *homosexual is forty-two years.* Paul Cameron, Ph.D., William Playfair, M.D., and Stephen Wellum, "The Longevity of Homosexuals: Before and After the Aids Epidemic," *Omega Journal of Death and Dying* 29, no. 3, 1994.

55 ... *partners during their lifetime.* Alan P. Bell, Martin S. Weinberg, *Homosexualities: A Study of Diversity among Men and Women* (New York: Simon and Schuster, 1978), 308–9.

55 ... *divorce rate estimated at 43 percent.* Robert Schoen, Robin M. Weinick, "The Slowing Metabolism of Marriage: Figures from 1988 U.S. Marital Status Life Tables," *Demography* 30, no. 2 (May 1993), 737–45.

55 ... *a husband or boyfriend?* In 1990, more than eight hundred women were killed by their husbands. Four hundred more were killed by their boyfriends. Antonia C. Novello, "From the Surgeon General, U.S. Public Health Service, a Medical Response to Domestic Violence," *Journal of the American Medical Association*, June 17, 1992, 3132.

56 ... *effective communicators of love.* Gary Chapman, *The Five Love Languages* (Chicago: Northfield Publishing, 1992), 15.

58 ... *speak at your event.* The author offers seminars for churches (www.lovinghomosexuals.com), and so does Focus on the Family (www.Lovewonout.com).

Chapter 3: The Homophobia Stops Here

64 ... *attraction to other men."* Gordon Dalbey, *Healing the Masculine Soul* (Waco: Word, 1988), 107.

66 ... *close quarters with homosexuals.* See George Weinberg, *Society and the Healthy Homosexual* (New York: St. Martins Press, 1972).

67 ... *cults extended their hands.* Joe Dallas, *Desires in Conflict* (Eugene, OR: Harvest House, 1991), 254.

69 ... *high school's nondiscrimination policy.* Mary Challender, "The Student Who Wouldn't Be Silent," *Des Moines Register*, May 6, 2002, 1E.

70 ... *to send in money.* Cal Thomas and Ed Dobson, *Blinded by Might* (Grand Rapids: Zondervan, 1999), 55.

77 ... *often show little grace.* Tim Stafford, "Ed Dobson Loves Homosexuals," *Christianity Today,* July 19, 1993, 22.

77 . . . *their scornful rejection instead.* Dalbey, *Healing the Masculine Soul,* 106.

78 . . . *one of those sins.* Steve Bush, *Rejecting Homosexuals,* compact disc (self-published, 2002). The quote is paraphrased from the CD.

78 . . . *so in Jesus' name.* Rob Marus, "Hatred in Jesus' Name," *Faithworks,* May–June 2000, 16.

79 . . . *sang of Jesus' love.* Philip Yancey, *What's So Amazing about Grace?* (Grand Rapids: Zondervan, 1997), 166.

80 . . . *realm of God's mercy.* Philip Yancey, *The Jesus I Never Knew* (Grand Rapids: Zondervan, 1995), 154–55.

80 . . . *matter infinitely to God.* Ibid., 159.

81 . . . *part of his name.* Ibid., 150.

81 . . . *crowd must have gasped.* Ibid., 172.

Chapter 4: A God Like Ours

84 . . . *ALL GAYS GO TO HELL.* John Paulk with Tony Marco, *Not Afraid to Change* (Mukilteo, WA: Winepress, 1998), 141.

86 . . . *to emerge looking good.* Kevin Jennings (speech to Human Rights Campaign, 1995). The speech was posted on, but has since been removed from, the GLSEN website.

86 . . . *take this project 24/7/365.* Stephen Bennett, responding to GLSEN's 2001 Day of Silence, as quoted on www.culture andfamily.com.

86 . . . *propaganda" in their schools.* Robert Knight, responding to GLSEN's 2001 Day of Silence, as quoted on www.culture andfamily.com.

88 . . . *with an ultrasound system.* Vicki Edwards, "A Picture's Worth" *The Lookout,* January 20, 2002, 7.

89 . . . *and fear" (emphasis added).* Mel White, *Stranger at the Gate* (New York: Penguin, 1994), 25.

89 . . . *a sexually oppressive subculture.* Michael Maudlin, "Scandal?" *Christianity Today,* August 14, 1995, 25.

92 . . . *37 percent had a friend who was lesbian or gay.* W. Throckmorton and G. Welton, *Are Christian College Students Homophobic?*

A White Paper Concerning Attitudes towards Homosexuals among Grove City College Students (Grove City, PA: Carolina Maud Publishing, 2003).

Chapter 5: What Does Science Say?

98 . . . *heterosexual and homosexual men.* Simon LeVay, "A Difference in Hypothalamic Structure between Heterosexual and Homosexual Men," *Science,* August 30, 1991, 1034.

98 . . . *twins and adopted brothers.* Bailey and Pillard, "A Genetic Study of Male Sexual Orientation," *Archives of General Psychiatry* 48 (1991), 1089.

98 . . . *and male sexual orientation.* Dean Hamer, "A Linkage between DNA Markers on the X Chromosomes and Male Sexual Orientation," *Science* 261 (July 16, 1993), 321.

98 . . . *some of his subjects.* Simon LeVay, "A Difference in Hypothalamic Structure," 1034.

99 . . . *behavioral and environmental conditions.* David Gelman, "Born or Bred?" *Newsweek* 119, no. 8 (February 24, 1992), 46.

99 . . . *in interpreting my work.* David Nimmons, "Sex and the Brain," *Discover* 15, no. 3 (March 1994), 64.

100 . . . *at twins raised apart.* Gelman, "Born or Bred?"

100 . . . *yield the discordant twins.* "Born or Bred?"

101 . . . *heard in the popular media.* See www.drthrockmorton.com.

102 . . . *homosexuality of his subjects.* John Horgan, "Gay Genes, Revisited: Doubts Arise over Research on the Biology of Homosexuality," *Scientific American* 273, no. 5 (November 1995), 26.

102 . . . *more complicated than that.* J. Madeleine Nash, "The Personality Genes," *Time* 151, no. 16 (April 27, 1998), 60.

102 . . . *toward a Gay Gene.* Jerry E. Bishop, "Research Points toward a Gay Gene," *Wall Street Journal,* July 16, 1993, B1.

102 . . . *Genetic Link to Homosexuality.* "Study Finds Genetic Link to Homosexuality," *Des Moines Register,* July 16, 1993, 6A.

102 . . . *its next manual (DSM III).* Charles W. Socarides, "Sexual Politics and Scientific Logic: The Issue of Homosexuality," *Journal of Psychohistory* 19, no. 3 (Winter 1992).

103 . . . *back into the DSM.* Ibid.

103 . . . *temper of the times.* Ronald Bayer, *Homosexuality and American Psychiatry: The Politics of Diagnosis* (New York: Basic Books, 1981), 3–4.

104 . . . *a very particular agenda.* Alix Spiegel, *81 Words,* radio production for National Public Radio.

104 . . . *successful treatment for it.* Joseph Nicolosi, *Reparative Therapy of Male Homosexuality* (Northvale, NJ: Aronson Books, 1997), 11.

105 . . . *efforts to heal it.* Gordon Dalbey, *Healing the Masculine Soul* (Waco: Word, 1988), 108.

105 . . . *Father God can heal.* Ibid., 109.

105 . . . *from gay to straight.* "Answers to Your Questions about Sexual Orientation and Homosexuality," www.APA.org/pubinfo/answers.html.

106 . . . *at the patient's request.* Jeffrey Satinover, M.D., *Homosexuality and the Politics of Truth* (Grand Rapids: Baker, 1996), 35–37.

106 . . . *sound bites to the public.* Jeffrey Satinover, M.D., *Journal of Human Sexuality* (1996), 8.

106 . . . *shaped at an early age.* American Psychological Association, *Answers to Your Questions about Sexual Orientation and Homosexuality,* www.APA.org/pubinfo/answers/html.

106 . . . *biological etiologies for homosexuality."* See www.psych.org/public_info/gaylesbianbisexualissues22701.pdf.

107 . . . *by God are legion.* Stanton L. Jones and Tim Stafford, "The Loving Opposition: Speaking the Truth in a Climate of Hate," *Christianity Today* 37, no. 8 (July 19, 1993), 18.

Chapter 6: What Causes Homosexuality?

110 . . . *that we are drawn.* Joseph Nicolosi, *Reparative Therapy of Male Homosexuality* (Northvale, NJ: Aronson Books, 1997), 186.

110 . . . *mother to the [father].* Ibid., 25–26.

111 . . . *another man can tell him.* Ibid., 154.

111 . . . *properly attained in childhood.* Andy Comiskey, "Healing the Child Within," *Desert Stream Newsletter,* January–February 1985, 2.

111 . . . *to an erotic one.* Ibid.

112 . . . *love through another woman.* Richard Cohen, *Coming Out Straight* (Winchester, VA: Oakhill Press, 2000), 26.

112 . . . *orientation. A 1994 questionnaire. Growing Up Gay,* an unpublished survey conducted in the Seattle area in 1994 by Correll and Carluzzi.

113 . . . *relationship with his father.* J. H. Brown, "Homosexuality as an Adaptation in Handling Aggression," *Journal of the Louisiana State Medical Society* 115, 304–11.

116 . . . *with men repulsive or frightening.* Dr. Carol Ahrens, Ph.D., in a chapter written for an older version of Joe Dallas's, *Desires in Conflict* (Eugene, OR: Harvest House, 1991), 193.

117 . . . *fit in with the jocks.* Jack Morlan, *Breaking the Chains* (self-published, 2002), 3.

118 . . . *appears to him, dangerously.* Nicolosi, *Reparative Therapy,* 58.

118 . . . *enjoyed playing sports "very much."* Peter Copeland and Dean Hamer, *The Science of Desire* (New York: Simon and Schuster, 1994), 167.

118 . . . *feminine activities during childhood.* Anne Paulk, *Restoring Sexual Identity* (Eugene, OR: Harvest House, 2003), 248.

Chapter 7: How Does Change Happen?

122 . . . *of the same sex.* Elizabeth Moberly, *Homosexuality: A New Christian Ethic* (Greenwood, SC: Attic Press, 1983), 42.

123 . . . *friendships with other men.* Was written in an email to the author.

123 . . . *masculinity or femininity respectively.* Gerard Van Den Aardweg, *Homosexuality and Hope: A Psychiatrist Talks about Treatment and Change* (Ann Arbor: Servant Books, 1986), 57.

124 . . . *source of maternal touch.* Dallas, *Desires in Conflict,* 200.

125 . . . *form of touch.* John Money and Anke A. Ehrhardt, *Man and Woman, Boy and Girl* (Baltimore: Johns Hopkins University Press, 1972), 132–3. See also Ray Raphael, *The Men from the Boys: Rites of Passage in Male America* (Lincoln: University of Nebraska Press, 1988).

125 . . . *the "body longing stage."* Gordon Dalbey, *Healing the Masculine Soul* (Waco: Word, 1988), 104.

125 . . . *all that: intimacy, closeness, connection.* John Eldredge, *Wild at Heart* (Nashville: Thomas Nelson, 2001), 120.

126 . . . *hard enough to cause fractures.* "Real Men Don't Hug Unless . . ." http://www.netpathway.com/%7Eccr/realmen.htm.

126 . . . *intimacy they were denied."* Mona Riley and Brad Sargent, *Unwanted Harvest* (Nashville: Broadman and Holman, 1995), 48.

128 . . . *brain, and so forth.* Gelman, "Born or Bred?" referring to Simon LeVay's research.

128 . . . *the course of treatment.* Joseph Nicolosi, *Reparative Therapy of Male Homosexuality* (Northvale, NJ: Aronson Books, 1997), 163.

129 . . . *was proud of me.* Riley and Sargent, *Unwanted Harvest,* 88.

132 . . . *Jesus' healing of someone.* See Matt. 9:21, Matt. 14:26, Mk. 3:10, Mk. 5:28, Mk. 6:56, Mk. 8:22, Mk. 10:13, Luke 6:19, and Luke 18:15.

134 . . . *a hug in church.* Philip Yancey, *What's So Amazing about Grace?* (Grand Rapids: Zondervan, 1997), 168.

135 . . . *substitute for [parents'] love.* Richard Cohen, *Coming Out Straight* (Winchester, VA: Oakhill Press, 2000), 72.

137 . . . *with a substitute parent.* Riley and Sargent, *Unwanted Harvest,* 47.

137 . . . *masculine vision and responsibility.* Ibid., 47–48.
137 . . . *failed father-son bond.* Nicolosi, *Reparative Therapy,* 150.
139 . . . *to play with me.* Ibid., 65.
139 . . . *an initiation into maleness?* Malcolm Boyd, *Take Off the Masks* (Philadelphia: New Society Publishers, 1984), 35.
139 . . . *they themselves feel deficient.* E. A. Kaplan, "Homosexuality: A Search for the Ego Ideal," *Archives of General Psychiatry* 16 (1967), 355–58.
140 . . . *for example, his "masculinity."* F. Weiss, "The Meaning of Homosexual Trends in Therapy: A Roundtable Discussion" (paper presented before the Association for the Advancement of Psychoanalysis, New York, January 1963).
142 . . . *maybe I am one after all.* Eldredge, *Wild at Heart,* 128.
142 . . . *that fosters male identification.* Nicolosi, *Reparative Therapy,* 188.
143 . . . *to know you better, follow through.* Joe Dallas, *Desires in Conflict* (Eugene, OR: Harvest House, 1991), 174.
144 . . . *those guys loved me.* Bob Davies, "Homosexuals and the Church," *Moody Magazine* 94, no. 9 (May 5, 1994), 12–18.
144 . . . *who is sexually attractive.* Nicolosi, *Reparative Therapy,* 120.
145 . . . *other men can teach him.* Ibid., 189.
147 . . . *a world involving danger.* Eldredge, *Wild at Heart,* 65.
149 . . . *others invariably shows up.* Dallas, *Desires in Conflict,* 149.
150 . . . *or even attempt suicide.* Private correspondence.
151 . . . *correctness of the times.* Ben Newman, *Anything but Straightforward: A Rebuttal to Wayne Besen,* www.peoplecanchange.com.
151 . . . *heterosexual attraction and functioning.* Ibid.
152 . . . *after counseling or therapy.* NARTH's 1997 Survey on Change, www.NARTH.com.
152 . . . *was finishing this book.* Robert L. Spitzer, "Can Some Gay Men and Lesbians Change Their Sexual Orientation? *Archives of Sexual Behavior* 32, no. 5 (October 2003), 403–17.
152 . . . *Professional Psychology: Research and Practice.* Warren Throckmorton, "Initial Empirical and Clinical Findings Concern-

ing the Change Process for Ex-Gays," *Professional Psychology: Research and Practice* 33 (June 2002), 242–48.

153 . . . *am preoccupied by them.* Nicolosi, *Reparative Therapy*, 166.

153 . . . *buzzing around my ear.* Ibid., 166.

154 . . . *and spiritual well-being.* Joseph Nicolosi et al., *Psychological Reports* (June 2000), 1078.

155 . . . *a perfectly worthy aim.* Camille Paglia, *Vamps and Tramps* (New York: Vintage Books, 1994), 77.

157 . . . *the same illusional way.* Nicolosi, *Reparative Therapy*, 200.

Afterword: Why Can't I Be Proud?

167 . . . *road to doing justice.* Mel White, *Stranger at the Gate* (New York: Penguin, 1994), 284.

Resources

Books

Dallas, Joe. *Desires in Conflict.* Eugene, OR: Harvest House, 1991.

Joe Dallas, a mental-health counselor who has overcome homosexuality, addresses the struggles of people with unwanted homosexual attractions. A great first book for someone seeking answers.

Cohen, Richard. *Coming Out Straight.* Winchester, VA: Oakhill Press, 2000.

Richard Cohen presents a model for change, coupled with stories of people who have overcome homosexuality. This book details some of the specific methods by which non-sexual touch can help individuals who are overcoming homosexuality. Note: The healing methods in this book are designed to take place between a homosexual struggler and his or her parents. Therapists should not hold their clients, nor should homosexual strugglers hold each other.

Eldredge, John. *Wild at Heart*. Nashville: Thomas Nelson, 2001.

This book is not written specifically about homosexuality; however, it describes many of the fears, insecurities, and questions that haunt every man and describes the road to wholeness. Naturally, many of the insights in the book can be valuable to someone who is in the process of overcoming homosexuality.

Konrad, Jeff. *You Don't Have to Be Gay*. Newport Beach, CA: Pacific Publishing House, 1987.

You Don't Have to Be Gay is a series of recorded letters between Jeff Konrad, a former homosexual, and a friend of his who initially believes that change is impossible. A great book for skeptics!

Nicolosi, Joseph. *Reparative Therapy of Male Homosexuality*. Northvale, NJ: Aronson, 1997.

Dr. Nicolosi describes the steps necessary to overcome homosexuality, as well as provides insights about motivations behind sexual behavior and issues from childhood. He also discusses how to deal with many of the issues that will surface in a relationship with a surrogate or a therapist, such as anger, dependency, and inferiority.

Nicolosi, Joseph and Linda Ames Nicolosi. *A Parent's Guide to Preventing Homosexuality*. Downer's Grove, IL: InterVarsity Press, 2002.

Dr. and Mrs. Nicolosi explain how parents can identify potential developmental problems in children, and give practical advice for addressing them. Critical reading for parents, teachers, and mental-health professionals.

Paulk, Anne. *Restoring Sexual Identity*. Eugene, OR: Harvest House, 2003.

Former lesbian Anne Paulk offers insights into the specific challenges faced by women who are in the process of overcoming homosexuality.

Satinover, Jeffrey. *Homosexuality and the Politics of Truth.* Grand Rapids: Baker Books, 1996.

Psychiatrist and author Jeffrey Satinover recounts his experiences with homosexual patients and examines the politics behind scientific research on sexual orientation.

(The following books are not about homosexuality, but they provide valuable insight into some of the evangelistic tools mentioned in this book.)

Ham, Ken. *Why Won't They Listen?* Green Forest, AZ: Master Books, 2002.

Ken Ham explains why he believes that refuting evolution is often necessary before one can experience success in sharing the gospel. He deftly points out the flaws in Darwinism and shows how Christian compromise in the areas of science and history will eventually destroy the church.

Richardson, Don. *Eternity in Their Hearts.* Ventura, CA: Regal Books, 1981.

Don Richardson explains that there is knowledge of God, even if it is incomplete, in the minds and cultures of social groups around the world. This book is a faith builder and a book of wisdom for all who would reach out to people with the gospel.

Yancey, Philip. *The Jesus I Never Knew.* Grand Rapids: Zondervan, 1995.

Respected Christian journalist Philip Yancey puts his preconceptions aside and attempts to take an objective look at the life of the man who forever changed human history. This book is highly recommended for anyone who desires to know more about the life of Jesus.

Websites

www.Christianaids.org

Lula M. Minor-Lofton, founder of the Christian Aids Outreach Ministry, Inc., is available to offer help and resources for those who have been affected by AIDS.

www.Crossministry.org

Resources for equipping the church to evangelize and disciple the homosexual.

www.Exodus.to

Exodus is the largest Christian referral and information center dealing with homosexual issus in the world. Exodus provides speakers, conferences, and a nationwide network of support groups for homosexual strugglers.

www.DrThrockmorton.com

Dr. Throckmorton is associate professor of psychology at Grove City College in Pennsylvania. He has done some excellent scientific research on homosexuality. He is also the producer of the ex-gay film *I Do Exist.*

www.Inqueery.com

Resources and research for addressing the issue of homosexuality in the public schools.

www.Family.org

Focus on the Family's website offers resources on overcoming homosexuality and many other topics of interest to Christians. Focus on the Family also offers referrals to counselors who help those overcoming homosexuality.

www.Gaytostraight.org

Website for the International Healing Foundation and Richard Cohen, M.A. An excellent resource for individuals seeking to overcome same-sex attractions.

www.NARTH.com

The National Association of Research and Therapy of Homosexuality (NARTH) is a scientific organization of professional therapists as well as laypeople in fields such as law, religion, and education. They offer referrals to counselors who help those overcoming homosexuality.

www.P-Fox.org

Website for Parents and Friends of Ex-Gays and Gays, an organization that offers help to parents and friends of homosexuals.

www.Realityresources.com

Jerry and Charlene Leach codirect an international ministry to those afflicted with homosexuality and transgenderism.

You may contact the author by email at chad@lovinghomosexuals.com. Though he may not be able to reply to every email, he would love to hear your thoughts on this book.